IT'S WHAT EDDIE DID

ROBERT PHILIP BOLTON

Also by Robert Philip Bolton
The Fable of Flitcroft Point
Jacko. One Bloke. One Year.
The Boys and Men of Auckland's Mickey Rooney Gang
The Fine Art of Kindness
Six Murders?
To The White Gate
Underneath The Arclight
My Marian Year
The Boltons of The Little Boltons
The Tapu Garden of Eden
For Viktor. The story of Mussorgsky's 'Pictures at an Exhibition'
The Collected Short Stories (in which is combined *Nana's Special Day and other stories, The Dolphin and other stories,* and *Quickies.*)

Robert Philip Bolton was born in New Zealand in 1945. He has been writing most of his adult life. Most of his work is about New Zealand and New Zealanders. He lives in Auckland.

IT'S WHAT EDDIE DID

Copyright © Robert Philip Bolton
ISBN: 978-0-473-68870-7 (Soft Cover)
ISBN: 978-0-473-68871-4 (Kindle)
Cover design: DIY Publishing.co.nz.

A note from the author

It's What Eddie Did is a work of fiction. Except for some historical events and real people referred to in passing, the events and characters in this story are entirely my own creation, the products of my imagination, based in part on my own experiences in the business of advertising. Pan American World Airways and N. W. Ayer were once active in New Zealand but neither business now exists anywhere in the world.

This book is dedicated to the partners, employees, clients and suppliers of MacHarman Associates

1

For Allison.

All right. Here we go. It's a nice day outside. I'm warm and comfortable. Got a cup of tea and a Mallow Puff. I'm doing this for Allison.

To start with, I was born on the twenty-first of April, nineteen twenty-six, the same day as the queen. When I was born my father had a good job as a printer at *The Auckland Star*. Mother, whose name was Winola but was always known as Winnie, came from a travelling German circus family. Evidently though she quickly settled into the life of a wife and mother in a typical New Zealand working-class household. Whenever she was asked about her exciting past as an acrobat, performing all over the world, she would say — in a strong German accent which she never lost and I never liked — I like it very much to be an ordinary Kiwi. She usually sounded less than convincing.

When he met mother my father had just turned twenty and was on apprentice wages. He was living with his older brother Toby and his wife as his parents had died in the nineteen eighteen flu epidemic. He'd gone to the circus at Western Springs with his new fiancé; I don't know anything about her. Anyway, towards the end of the programme, when the German circus band was playing at its most raucous and dissonant, he had fallen hopelessly in love, across the sawdusty horse-shitty ground of the circus ring, with the pretty little blonde and smiling *Fraulein* who, in the climax of her family's remarkable act, climbed up the muscular, quivering and sweating bodies of her parents, brothers and sister, aunts, uncles and cousins, to top off the world famous Zumpe Human Pyramid.

She was very beautiful — so I was told and easily believed — in her dark yellow leotard, trimmed with red fringing; and so powerful was her attraction to the young apprentice printer that he abandoned his fiancé to run outside, frantically searching around the big top, checking all the other tents and caravans, asking random circus hands, who couldn't speak English anyway, for guidance, hoping desperately to find the little German teenager who, he was already convinced, would one day be his wife.

My father told me all this when I was a child and he was still young, employed and sober.

Meanwhile Winola Elsa Zumpe — for that was the full name of the beautiful young *acrobatiste* — was forced to continue with her family on the circus's eternal global journey. But she and my father kept in touch by letter — she had passable English even then — until, eventually, in an unbearable longing to be with her handsome young Kiwi, she ran away from her family while the circus was performing in Southern Rhodesia. In Cape Town — she herself told me the story — she stowed away on a steamer bound, via Melbourne, for Auckland where she and my father were married in the Auckland Registry Office; my Uncle Toby and Aunt Edith were witnesses. Mother had just turned eighteen but the registrar accepted her father's letter of consent — which she herself had forged on circus paper — as it was written in German and neither he nor his officials wanted to admit they knew nothing of that despised language.

Three children and a new home.

That was in nineteen twenty-three when, after the Great War, there was a lot of anti-German sentiment. As a result, mother, who loved her new country, was not only glad to be rid of her German surname — although she could never shake off her accent — but also insisted, when a baby was born the next year, that she should have a real English-sounding name: Doris.

When I was born, two years later, my father wanted to call me Max after his own father who was named Maxwell Edward, but mother resisted. Max means Maximillian, she said, which is too much German. *Klingt zu Deutsch*. I do not like it. But it's after my father, said my father. He was *Maxwell*, not Maximillian. Maxwell and Max are perfectly ordinary English names. This I do not know but I do not care a fig, said mother adamantly. He's not going to be Max and that's the end of it. But that wasn't exactly the end of it. In the end I was called Edward Maxwell, my grandfather's names in reverse, although I've always been called just plain Eddie.

Eddie Purvis. That's me.

As much as I can remember my infant years were idyllic. Mother adored her children and, cut off from her constantly travelling German family, who had disowned her anyway, she poured all her love into looking after us. Everything she did — the most mundane and routine housekeeping and motherly chores — she did willingly, gladly, happily, with love, so devoted was she to our welfare. She was, in fact, a truly wonderful mother.

My father, so in love with his beautiful young German bride, continued to enjoy his work. His apprenticeship was completed in due course and so his wages increased accordingly. He was considered a good and loyal employee and an expert operator of the paper's giant presses. On the strength of his job security and increased wages he bought a modern three-bedroom villa in Mackelvie Street, Grey Lynn. It was there mother established a happy and secure home for her family which increased by one in July nineteen twenty-eight. Catherine-Ann was chosen as a suitably non-German-sounding name for the new baby girl whose premature birth meant she was small, underweight and frail. Her indifferent health always demanded special care and attention from her young and now-worried mother.

I had no interest in the new baby but I adored Doris, my senior by two years. When I was five I followed her to Newton Central school after the May holidays of nineteen thirty-one.

The Great Depression and poverty.

Meanwhile a dark cloud of gloom — they called it 'The Great Depression' — quickly spread around the world. Few New Zealand families escaped its privations and some — the Purvis family of Grey Lynn included — were affected more than most.

At the end of that year, my first year at school, my father had his wages cut by a quarter. It was a fate shared by most of his colleagues and many other working-class men. Mother, and many thousands of housewives like her, suddenly discovered how helpless she was in the face of a global depression. Through no fault of our own we were suddenly and literally *poor*.

Caring only to keep us well fed, clothed, warm, healthy and secure, mother soon found that my father's reduced wages were not enough, that sacrifices and economies were necessary, and that suddenly the world was a scary and threatening place. And my father, unable to meet his building society obligations, had to sell the Mackelvie Street house where we had been so happy. He told us, angrily, that a rich man from Remuera got another bargain house to rent. We — including sickly little Catherine-Ann — had to shift to a cheap rental in Freeman's Bay. It was an old, cold and draughty two-storied wooden house, a virtual hovel, with an outside lean-to sleep-out shed for a bedroom, an outdoor toilet and no hot water. We had to share the house with the Gourleys, a meek middle-aged couple, in similarly straitened circumstances, who took the upper floor.

I was not quite six at Christmastime, nineteen thirty-one, but I easily remember it as a sombre celebration in our gloomy new home in Georgina Street. Mother did her best to create a happy atmosphere and make a good Christmas dinner from mutton chops, potatoes from the back yard vegetable garden which my father and his fellow tenant had inherited, and the puha which they found growing wild and plentiful against the back boundary fence.

Next Christmas we'll have chicken for dinner, said mother who had been given some yellow chicks by Mrs Parāone in Elizabeth Street. Imagine it, she said in German. Delicious roast chicken. We've got all year to fatten them up with scraps. And we'll soon have fresh eggs too. And fresh vegetables, added my father, trying to be jolly. But he found it hard to be cheerful when all he could afford for my Christmas present was a cheap pencil case, with a pencil and rubber, for my new school — Napier Street — where I would be starting in February.

My father's downfall.
Despite mother's brave cheerfulness, put on I suppose

for our sake, my father was becoming bitter and resentful. But you should be glad to have a job, said mother when I heard them arguing. Many men here, around the world, have no work. I read it. In your own paper even. They are much poorer than us. Their little ones go hungry. All over the world the same. Even in Deutschland. It is causing much trouble there. That man, Herr Hitler, a great troublemaker. So, we are lucky for sure.

At the beginning of nineteen thirty-two my father got caught up in a violent riot in Queen Street. Thousands of men, mostly unemployed, angry and hungry, had marched up Queen Street in protest, looting shops as they went. He wasn't arrested, as many were, but he arrived home drunk, late that night, with torn clothes, a blackened eye and a battery-operated portable radio looted from some shop.

That, as I recall, was the beginning of my father's downfall and failure as a husband and father. He'd probably began drinking in a vain attempt to relieve his understandable depression; his late-night arguments with mother often kept me and Doris awake.

At last, just before Christmas, nineteen thirty-two, he got the sack for drunkenness. A danger to himself and others, they said. Supervising those massive presses requires total sobriety, they said. I heard him telling Uncle Toby. I told them to get rooted, he said.

Despite having roast chicken for Christmas in nineteen thirty-two, as mother had promised in nineteen thirty-one, it was another miserable day due to a tragedy earlier that year from which mother never fully recovered.

A family tragedy.
It was in the winter of that year, nineteen thirty-two —

July — after the riot but before my father lost his job, that little Catherine-Ann was admitted to Princess Mary children's hospital suffering from a mysterious and wasting disease. 'Failure to thrive' they said. She died there, alone, a few days after her fourth birthday.

The effect on my parents was devastating. I didn't understand it then but their grief, and its long-term effects, must have been obvious to anyone. I know now that a tragedy like that can bring grieving parents together, but it wasn't like that for them. My father was so stricken that he couldn't express himself to anyone let alone to his lovely and still-young wife. And so, emotionally crippled, he gradually removed himself from family life — mentally if not physically — and took even more to the drink. And he didn't complain — couldn't be bothered I suppose — when mother insisted that he install another bed in my lean-to sleep-out.

Depressed and unemployed, with no options, but constrained, I suppose, by his latent decency, my father became a dutiful but distant husband and father. Meanwhile mother became cold and remote to the husband she had once loved enough to leave her family. Having lost little Catherine-Ann so tragically, and without the support of her husband or any of her own kin, she became chronically anxious and began to treat me and Doris as precious and fragile. We had to learn to live with a remote, frequently drunk, moody and evidently uncaring father, and a fretful, overprotective and doting mother whose nervous disposition — I realized this only later — was unconsciously transferred to poor Doris.

I was at school the day Catherine-Ann died. I'd never had much to do with her; she was just my sick little sister who commanded too much of mother's time and attention. It seemed to me then — when she died —

that family life returned to 'normal'. To say I was glad when she died would be wrong but it would be right enough to say I wasn't really sad either. And the fact that my father was now sleeping in my bedroom was something I didn't question.

Unwilling to divorce or even separate — a financial impossibility then — my parents must have agreed to live together and behave as if they were a normal, happy couple with two lovely children. It was a charade that wouldn't have fooled anyone. And if we — Doris and I — didn't see through it then, being too young, we could easily sense the tense and unhappy atmosphere in which we spent the rest of our childhood.

My friend Willy.

The dreary years of the early nineteen-thirties passed uneventfully for me. Despite starting a new school together, Doris and I soon drifted apart. She fell in with a set of Pākehā girls although she didn't play with them outside school. I thought they were snobby.

Although Doris was a good student, quiet, shy and compliant, she didn't like school. She much preferred to be home helping mother with female domestic chores. Unlike me, she harboured a deep sadness about the death of little Catherine-Ann whom she had loved dearly. And she tried but couldn't relieve the sadness she also sensed in mother. Over the next few years Doris gradually became more fretful and nervous, shy and timid. I loved her as a sister but wished she wasn't always sad.

I preferred to ignore family problems and tensions. Even at that young age I consciously decided to get on with life without inhibition. I enjoyed my new school and made many friends, mostly Māori boys. Freeman's Bay was a mostly Māori and poor enclave at that time.

One boy, Willy Parāone, the son of mother's new chicken-keeping friend, who lived around the corner in Elizabeth Street, was destined to be a lifelong friend. Willy was a lot like me: self-confident, independent and quick-witted, with a cleverness that bordered on cunning. Neither of us was taxed by our school lessons so we often became bored and troublesome.

Mother, overwhelmed by melancholia after Catherine-Ann's death, concentrated all her energy on keeping her part of our shared house clean and tidy, using all her wiles to stretch her housekeeping budget to provide us with enough nourishing food. My father though had almost given up on parenthood. He was on a pitiful benefit of some kind for almost a year after his humiliating sacking from the paper until his brother — my Uncle Toby — using his influence somewhere, found him a job as a gardener at the zoo in Westmere. His dignity and income somewhat restored, he seemed to reduce his drinking. I remember him coming home drunk only once or twice a week.

While my parents lived together in virtual misery, and Doris's sadness seemed to increase, I treated the shared Georgina Street house as no more than a base from which to launch myself into the life I wanted; a life of fun, pleasure, activity, optimism and, above all, free of poverty and sadness. I was convinced I was different from my parents and sister: they were so gloomy and pessimistic while I felt, what? optimistic; positive; energetic; anxious to get on with life. It occurred to me that as I was so 'different' from them I was possibly, probably, adopted. Even a bit Māori. I told Willy that and he rightly laughed at the idea based on the visible evidence.

I spent all my spare time with Willy.

My parents continued to do their duty — to each

other and their children — clinging somewhat hopelessly to their idea of family life, but I literally shrugged off any show of affection from mother or attempted discipline from my father. I was determined to be independent; to depend on no one for anything. And yet, despite my taller-than-average height, and my strutting bravado — an amusing act really — I was, nevertheless, as nineteen thirty-five ended, a poor and simple boy, of average intelligence, approaching my tenth birthday.

Much to the annoyance of our frustrated young teacher, Willy and I ended our standard three year by managing to pass — just — all the tests she set for the class. Nineteen thirty-six and the fourth standard awaited.

Willy and the school holidays.

But first, the holidays. I was rarely home during that long summer holiday. Where I went and what I did was both a mystery and a worry to mother although my father — who himself sometimes spent more time at *The Suffolk* than he did at home — dismissed my day-long absences with a casual and often intoxicated 'boys will be boys'.

Why can't he be like Doris? mother would ask. Doris helps me at home all the time. Woman's work, said my scornful father. But he, said mother, referring to me, is gone all day. With that Willy boy. Doing *what?* Doing mischief I think. But my father wasn't concerned. They're young lads in their summer holidays, Win, he said. Having freedom and fun. Who can blame them? After all, boys will be boys. Make the most of it is what I say.

Many of our summer adventures were at nearby Shelly Beach, by the seaside swimming baths, where the harbour bridge is now. In the beginning, before Christmas, we found a dinghy there, stored upside down, with a pair of oars inside. If the tide was in we took to rowing — a skill we taught ourselves — along the coast to Cox's Bay; we even rowed out to Watchman Island. We were careful to leave the dinghy exactly how and where we found it so as to not alert the unknown owner. It must have worked as it was always there next time.

Sometimes, when the weather was really hot, we'd run down to the ferry buildings, staying in the shade of the shop verandas to avoid the hot tar burning our bare feet, and hitch a ride to Devonport on one of the big steam ferries. There we'd walk around to Cheltenham Beach to swim in our underpants. We also climbed to the top of Mount Victoria before moving to North Head to explore its Māori caves and abandoned military tunnels.

In those days it took thirty-minutes to get to Devonport. At first we had to move around the deck ahead of or behind the ticket collector. It wasn't hard to sneak on, in Auckland and Devonport, but getting off at each end, jumping from the slippery deck rail to the wharf, was dangerous. One kindly captain, manoeuvring into position beside the Devonport wharf, saw us from his wheelhouse and told the crew to 'let those two rascals on and off whenever they like'. After that the Devonport trips weren't so much fun.

We often went to the daytime pictures thanks to Uncle Toby. We acted innocently although I knew exactly what we were doing when we marched into the 'T. Purvis, Watchmaker & Jeweller' shop in Queen Street. I knew my kindly uncle would give us sixpence each — enough to go to the pictures and buy an ice cream — just to get rid of us.

Summer humiliation at Brown's Bay.

It was thanks to Uncle Toby I once had a camping holiday at faraway Brown's Bay where I later owned a lot of land. We — me and Doris, eavesdropping together — heard Uncle Toby telling his brother, loudly and angrily, that our mother was in danger of suffering a 'nervous breakdown' after the death of Catherine-Ann, that he himself was at risk from drinking too much, that his nervy little daughter Doris spent too much time indoors, was looking pale, and needed some fresh air and sunshine, and that young Eddie — me — was running wild on the city streets with that grubby little Māori kid getting up to God-knows-what.

The thing is, Quentin, we heard him say, you're all in need of a good holiday at the beach. Come Christmas you can stay in my caravan at Brown's Bay for a couple of weeks. That was in the summer holidays of nineteen thirty-four/thirty-five. It was only a fortnight but it refreshed us all, exactly as Uncle Toby had hoped.

However, it was there and then I finally knew — no doubt about it — that my father no longer cared for me even a little. It was a hot, sunny afternoon on New Year's Day, nineteen thirty-five, when I was left standing in the middle of the Brown's Bay camping ground, holding a rugby ball on my hip — I didn't even like rugby — watching my father turn away and stroll off across the field to meet someone. I was puzzled; mildly embarrassed. I looked around to see if anyone had noticed my humiliation but they were all — including mother — too busy annual-holidaying at the beach to notice one small boy's disappointment. I stood there for a moment, thinking. That was very good, Eddie, is what I wanted to hear. I never knew you could kick a ball so high and catch so good. Do it again, papa, I said. Kick it to me again. I can do it even better. No, said my father,

I've got to go. Where? Where are you going? Can I come? No, said my father angrily. Go back to the caravan, boy. To your mother. But, papa, I pleaded, *please* can I go with you. But that made him angrier. He stopped. Go back, he shouted, pointing. Your mother wants you. It'll be lunch soon. But, papa, where are you going? I asked again. But my father didn't answer. He just turned and walked off as if I weren't there.

A working-class celebration. And a memorable birthday.
Later, in November that year, nineteen thirty-five, there was a morning of rare joy for my joyless father. Mr and Mrs Gourley came downstairs to celebrate the victory of the Labour Party in the general election. At last, said Mr Gourley. Those Tories are gone at last. And about bloody time, said my father. Here's to Mr Savage, he said as he raised a morning glass of beer. Things will change now.

But 'things' didn't change, didn't improve, at least not for a while, and certainly not for the residents of thirty-one Georgina Street. And then, suddenly, it was the twenty-first of April, nineteen thirty-six, my tenth birthday. The first birthday I *really* remember because of the present I got.

I remember waking up that morning, sitting up in bed, looking about expectantly, hoping to find some sort of present somewhere. I looked hopefully to the end of the bed but there was nothing there. I looked across the room and noticed that my father's bed looked unslept in which seemed odd to me. Then I saw a parcel sitting on my side of the apple box which stood between the two beds. It was only small. I didn't know what to expect — hardly dared to expect anything — but I hadn't imagined anything quite so mysteriously small, long, narrow and thin.

I pushed back the blankets, got up and crossed the small room to pull aside the curtain — it was a flour sack with blue and red printing — to let in more light. I was glad to see it wasn't raining for my birthday. Anyway, I sat on the edge of the bed, in my pyjamas, with the little parcel. It was wrapped in coarse brown paper and tied with thin twine knotted in a loose bow. I pulled at the bow, tore away the twine and paper to reveal a little chocolate-brown box with a gold crest on the lid. I remember lifting the snug-fitting lid and gasping in pleasant surprise.

I got a watch for my tenth birthday. A smart *Bifora* watch with a brown leather strap.

But as I was always being told we were poor I wondered how we could have afforded such a wonderful gift. It must have cost at least five pounds as I'd seen the posters at Uncle Toby's shop: *Bifora. The best buy for a fiver.*

I took it out of the box, tried the winder but found it was almost fully wound, and so strapped it around my thin wrist. It was a miniature version of a man's watch. It even had a luminous dial.

I went to the kitchen. Doris was there, at the table, eating toast spread with dripping and jam. Where's dad? I asked mother; she was at the sink, washing dishes. He had to go to work early, she said. I knew he never went to work early and that his bed hadn't even been slept in but I said nothing about that. Instead I said: But it's my birthday, mama. I stretched out my left arm and pushed up my pyjama sleeve. I want to thank him for my watch. It's neat.

Mother turned and smiled weakly. *Du solltest deinem Onkel Toby danken,* she said even though she knew I hated her speaking German. Uncle Toby? I asked. Really? My mother could have pretended; I'm sure

Uncle Toby wouldn't have minded. But, no, mother couldn't do that; she couldn't lie.

Yes, she said in English. It's from your Uncle Toby.

2

The end of primary school; haera rā, Willy.

My last years at Napier Street primary were not happy. For one thing I lost my best friend Willy when Mrs Parāone decided that city life was bad for him. He was sent away to the country to live with whānau. Where exactly? I asked. Willy didn't know. It's just a place up north, he said. A country town. A marae. By a river. They say I'm not Māori enough, eh, so I have to go and live with my auntie.

Other school friends were lost when their financially stressed parents took them out of school. The class in my standard six year, nineteen thirty-eight, was half the number of the year before. Boys and girls were being sent out to work at just twelve or thirteen years old, for pitiful staving-off-starvation wages, for the sake of their families. Government truant officers were routinely told to 'bugger off' by anxious parents.

Doris was old enough to leave school so was sent, by our sad and reluctant mother, to work as a live-in maid to skivvy for the rich Brinnerman family in Epsom for no more than a few shillings a week. But mother made me stay at school until the end of my standard six year, and then go to high school, despite the expense of feeding and clothing a growing boy. By then I knew for certain what I had always suspected: that I wasn't especially clever but that my mind worked differently — more quickly — and retained more, than any of my contemporaries and many adults including my father and some teacher dullards. I hoped high school would be more challenging.

My first job. Earning money at The Auckland Star.
I missed Willy during the long summer holiday before secondary school. I thought I was too old to fill the empty days on my own, the way I used to with Willy, so I was glad when my father used his union contacts to get me a job at the *Star.*

Six afternoons a week I helped load the paper's first edition onto trucks. The papers — still sticky with ink — came off the high-speed rotary presses at Fort Street and, wire-bound in heavy bundles, tumbled down the chute to the cart dock and the waiting trucks. And then, standing on the back of one of the trucks, I helped deliver them to the paper boys waiting on key Queen Street intersections. As the afternoon wore on I was back at the cart dock helping load the late afternoon and evening editions for the suburbs where squadrons of boys with special canvas bags slung over the bar of their bicycles would set about delivering the ink-smudged *Auckland Star* to its many thousands of news-starved readers.

And what gloomy news it was. It seemed the world was doomed to go to war. But during that summer I cared more about the money I earned as well as the satisfaction I got from hard work, mixing with printers, labourers, carriers, clerks and other boys, unaware that one day I would be an important advertising client of that influential newspaper. At that time I was no more than a cheap young labourer.

As I worked that summer, before I started high school, I knew I was putting childhood behind me; I was becoming a man. And I was saving money. I got paid for my holiday job on Thursdays. I gave two-and-six to mother. The next afternoon, before work, I stopped in at the Auckland Savings Bank's head office in Queen Street — it's a McDonald's now — where I banked the rest of my small wage but for a couple of shillings for a fortnightly haircut and a weekly visit to the pictures with Doris and mother.

We avoided the Queen Street theatres preferring the Britannia in Ponsonby and the Avon in Great North Road, because they were much cheaper. I really liked saving money, see. I liked seeing my bank balance grow. And, unlike most boys of my generation, I avoided the expensive habit of smoking.

Discovering a talent at high school.

When I started high school, at the beginning of nineteen thirty-nine, I thought I'd probably follow my father into the printing trade; Seddon Tech in Wellesley Street had a print shop with an excellent reputation. But one master, and one period, in just the first week at my new school, revealed a native talent which surprised me. And when it happened I instantly, without hesitation or doubt, knew what I wanted to do for a job.

Thanks to my art teacher — Mr Roper — I discovered I could draw exceptionally well with almost no training. I could draw anything — flora and fauna, landscapes, industrial machinery, cars and trucks, trains and planes, buildings and bridges, the human figure, faces, fingers, jewellery, fashion, anything — with an uncanny and astonishing accuracy in any medium on any surface. And although Mr Roper guided me through every aspect of my subject — including pencil, pen and ink drawing, charcoal drawing, painting with wash, watercolours and pastels, and oils on canvas, as well as the applied arts of silk-screening, printmaking and photography — I decided that drawing with pencil, pen and ink, together with a monochrome wash, was not only easy to master but could also lead to a job as a commercial artist.

Although my classes included an appreciation of the fine arts, I had no interest in either art history (the 'masters') or pursuing the *avant-garde,* believing from my studies that most 'art for art's sake' artists lived the same life of poverty I was determined to escape.

The world at war.

The world was at war before my first high school year was over. It didn't affect me. The army had encouraged the formation of a school cadet force of senior boys but I was too young in my first year.

My father, being only as old as the century, was required to register for military service. He said he was willing, even anxious, to serve, probably seeing it as an escape from his unhappy home life, but he was never called up. He *was* interviewed but was rejected due (officially) to his borderline age and an unspecified ear infection. I suspected later that his reputation for drunkenness had preceded him and thwarted his plans for escape to war although I heard him say that having a German wife was no help. They think I wouldn't want to kill Germans, he said.

My father's resentment at his rejection was reinforced when he learned, from his chapel friends at the *Star,* that many of his former senior colleagues and most of his young colleagues — even apprentices — had already been called up. He returned, disappointed, to his job at the zoo.

At school I was excelling at my favourite subject showing, according to Mr Roper's reports: '...a remarkable natural talent and aptitude which cannot be taught but which I can only strive to polish'. I didn't ignore my academic subjects, which I always managed to pass, just, but despite the school's reputation for sports, especially rugby and cricket, I didn't (then or ever) have any interest in team games or sports of any kind. Even then I suppose I was a bit of a loner.

War continued in Europe and the Middle East during my three years at secondary school. And despite the fact that we had regular school drills, in case of invasion, and had formed our own small 'army', and that my resentful father went out most nights wearing a Home Guard brassard over his old sports coat, I was hardly touched by the war.

My first 'proper' job.

At the end of nineteen forty-one, by which time I had passed my matriculation and left school to get back to my school holiday job at the *Star,* the Japs had launched a surprise bombing attack on the American navy base at Pearl Harbour in Hawaii as well as other air attacks on British territories in Malaya, Singapore and Hong Kong.

'JAPAN DECLARES WAR ON BRITAIN AND AMERICA' said the bold headline on the *Star's* page seven, the main news page, on Monday the eighth of December that year. This brought about the immediate and fateful entry of the United States into the war and, before long, a strong and unavoidable presence of the American military in Auckland. Most visible to me was the American camp being assembled on Victoria Park which I passed each morning and afternoon on my way to and from my first proper but very short-lived job.

It was 'proper' job thanks to my father again who still

knew plenty of folk in the printing trades; a five-year apprenticeship as a photo-engraver with a small firm in Federal Street called Printers Plate Processors Limited. But I wasn't signed up immediately; a three-month probation was customary to protect both parties. But I needed no more than three *days* — not three months — to know that working with stinking and corrosive chemicals in an old factory in Federal Street, with a motley collection of men too old or unfit for war, was not for me. At the end of my third day I walked out of Printers Plate Processors Limited and never returned.

Stupid bugger, said my father. Is good, said mother. All those chemicals is not good for young boy. Never did me no harm, said my father. You're an old man, said my mother to her husband who was then only forty-two years old.

Well, I'm never going to work in a factory, I said. So what are you going to do, boy? asked my angry father. You can't bludge off us all your bloody life. I won't bludge, I protested. I'd *never* bludge. Off you or anyone, you bastard. Don't fight, cried mother. Please. I stormed out of the house then, angry and frustrated, as my father yelled after me: So what are you going to do, you arrogant young prick?

What I *did* do, eventually, surprised everyone including myself.

Leaving home.
Before I left home, on that warm summer evening at the beginning of February, nineteen forty-two, having abandoned the chance of a secure trade — swearing I'd *never* bludge off my father or anyone — I went to Doris's bedroom and left a note under her pillow to find when she came home to sleep on Saturday night.

Why do they fight so? Doris asked me when we met

at the Three Lamps tram stop the following Sunday night; she was returning to her live-in job in Epsom. They just seem to hate each other. All parents fight all the time, I said. It's just normal. No it's not, insisted Doris. The Brinnermans never fight. They're happy and loving all the time. To each other and their little children. Maybe it's because they're rich, I said. Well, they're definitely *very* rich, said Doris. That's it then, I said. No money worries, nothing to fight about.

Where are you staying? Doris asked but I said only that she shouldn't worry about me. But mama's worried about you, said Doris. And she's so sad about Catherine-Ann. Do you think about Catherine-Ann? she asked with an accusing stare and quizzical frown. No, I said bluntly. Oh, I do, said Doris sadly. Ever so much. I even dream about her. All the time. It's not fair. Makes mama so sad.

You really should go and see mama, insisted Doris. I'm not there and she needs you. I will one day, I said. When *he's* not there. He's just a bloody old drunk. Well do be careful, said Doris as her tram arrived, grinding to a stop. I'll be all right, Dossy, I said as she stood at the top of tram steps and gave me a girly fingers-only wave. Just you see, I said. Just you see.

Kind Mrs Parāone's advice.

Meanwhile, unknown to my worried mother, who had no idea where I was or what I was doing, I had taken some clothes and my sketch pad, pencil set, pens and Indian inks, brushes and ceramic palette, up the road, to the Parāone house in Elizabeth Street, where I was welcomed without question by Willy's fat and loving mother. You stay here as long as you like, she said. Willy will be home soon. (Mr Parāone, an officer in the Māori Battalion, was away at war somewhere.) He'll be glad to see you, boy.

Without a job, without an income, I was starting to eat into my savings as I had to pay Mrs Parāone something for my board. I knew I could probably get back the part-time job at the *Star* but I guessed my father would find out as he still had chapel friends at the paper. I had no regrets about leaving the factory job but I wished I could get a job using my drawing ability.

I was often bored and so walked around town, my sketch pad and pencils in my old school bag, looking for a variety of subjects to draw. I was putting together a portfolio that would show my artistic versatility as well as my ability.

My ambition was to be a commercial artist. I saw my three years of high school art as an apprenticeship which qualified me as a tradesman who would, like any tradesman, be well paid for my training and skill. I was interested only in earning as much money as possible, as quickly as possible, for doing something I found remarkably easy: creating realistic and accurately detailed illustrations of anything or anyone, using paper, pencils, ink and wash, the simplest of a tradesman's tools. But how and where should I start?

I had no idea.

A few days later Mrs Parāone told me she had a letter from Willy which said he wasn't coming back to Auckland; that he liked it on the marae and working on his uncle's farm, that he was working hard, getting real fit, and was almost fluent in Māori. Thank Our Lord Jesus, said his mother.

He says here, she continued, reading from the open letter, that he'll probably see us at Christmas and that he hopes… well, the rest of it doesn't matter to you. The thing is, boy, he's not coming home no more.

I was, and must have looked, terribly disappointed, as she said: I'm sorry, Eddie. I know you were looking forward to seeing Willy again. You're still welcome here, you know, but this isn't *really* the place for you. This isn't your home. You should be with your mother. She's a good woman, boy. Be with her.

Confused, disappointed that I wouldn't be seeing Willy until Christmas — probably, he said — I just shrugged.

Families, Pākehā and Māori, continued Mrs Paraone. Some are happy. Some are sad. Some fight and argue. Some don't. There's no rules, boy. Your father has problems with the waipiro, eh. (Mrs Paraone's conversations were always laced with Māori words, like mother and her German.) Everyone knows. Is a worry for your mother. Feel sorry for her, eh. And your big sister. Always looks so sad. And the poor little tamāhine. So, you're welcome here, boy, you know that. But, really, your mother needs you, eh.

I knew she was right.

Returning home to problems. On my birthday.

The next morning — which happened to be my birthday — I walked down Elizabeth Street, turned left and walked two houses down Georgina Street to number thirty-one, the house — the big shabby two-storied rented house that my family shared with Mr and Mrs Gourley — which had been my home since the end of nineteen thirty-one. When I walked into the kitchen I found mother sitting at the table sobbing into a handkerchief.

Mama, I said quietly. She looked up then, saw me — it took her a moment to register that it really was me — and rushed into my arms, clinging to me, her head turned to one side and pressed against my chest. She seemed so small; tiny even.

Mama, I said. What is it? What's the matter? Oh, Eddie, my dear son, she said in German. To come home on your birthday. Sixteen already, today. I can't believe it. *Es tut mir leid, mein Sohn,* she added, being sorry she couldn't buy me a present. Mama, I said, my birthday doesn't matter. But what's wrong? It's your *Vater,* she said with a sniff. I pushed her back a little and asked: What about him? She looked up at me with wet and red eyes. He's in the hospital, she said.

I was astonished at this unexplained news. I steered mother back to her chair at the big kitchen table, sat down beside her, and listened to the story which she related, calmly, while anxiously wringing her handkerchief.

Evidently, two days before, my father had been found unconscious in an alley behind *The Rising Sun* in Karangahape Road. Obviously drunk, he had been beaten up and robbed of his tobacco, papers and matches, and the few pence he carried. A policeman had shown no interest — thinking him a tramp — but an ambulance had been called by someone. He was recovering in Auckland hospital.

He's all right really, said mother. I saw him last night. He'll be home later. I should get a taxi for him but there's no money. He'll have to walk all that way, over Grafton Bridge, on his crutches. But, oh, Eddie, also, he lost his job at the zoo for his drinking, and now this. We have no money. No savings. I don't know what to do. I was surprised then. Mother had never confided in me about my father or their lack of money.

I've got money for a taxi, I said.

There's something else, said mother looking up at me and evidently seeing a man she could trust: a boy no longer. Her eyes were red rimmed and her cheeks were wet and blotchy with tears, and she held her damp handkerchief up to her mouth. What? I asked. What else? The war, she said. The awful war. The people don't like me anymore. What people? I asked. The men, and ladies too, in the Three Lamps shops, she said. The butcher and baker. The men in the Four Square. And Mr Sutcliffe in the fruit shop. And his wife. Mr White the chemist. Even that new lady in the dairy. The people in Ponsonby — in the whole country — they don't like *Deutsche Leute*. And they know I'm one of them, Eddie: a hated German. But, mama, no, I protested although I knew it was true. It's true, Eddie, she said. Ask your father. He knows. Everyone knows. It's awful.

Later that afternoon I collected my clothes, few belongings, drawing materials and portfolio from the Parāone house and moved back to the lean-to sleep-out I would again have to share with my depressed and evidently ailing father. I had picked him up from the hospital, with mother, in a taxi which only I could afford. When we got home my father thanked me sullenly before stumbling to his bed and falling asleep. I assumed he had forgotten my birthday.

How's your father? mother asked when I returned to the kitchen. Asleep, I said. The poor man, she said. I shrugged. I cared little for my drunken father who didn't even know what day it was. In fact right then I cared only about getting a job as an artist.

Unfortunately I still had no idea how and where to start.

3

Thanks to Uncle Toby.

I learned later that my sturdy and reliable little *Bifora* watch — which I wore for years — was only the tip of the financial support iceberg that was my Uncle Toby. It seems he often provided financial support to his younger brother's family. Evidently he had come to admire and respect his sister-in-law for her loyalty to her hopeless husband and the care she lavished on her two remaining children. But it wasn't just financial support; Doris told me later that he thought that she, Doris, shouldn't have to work as a Brinnermans' live-in servant. In those days she always looked so pale, Uncle Toby told me much later. So withdrawn and timid, he said, and badly wounded by the death of her little sister.

He knows Mr Brinnerman, said an excited Doris, and he doesn't like him one little bit.

Uncle Toby somehow got Doris a job at McKenzie's in Karangahape Road where her mild manner and gentle nature, and her speed with mentally calculating change, were valued by the store manager. Mother was thrilled to have Doris home again; I was there when she thanked Uncle Toby.

Uncle Toby also used his influence to ensure that I —

young and strong — replaced my dismissed father at the zoo. It was a physical, outdoor job which I thoroughly enjoyed and where I was liked by my colleagues and superiors for the strength, energy and even temperament my father had lacked. I spent my lunch times and breaks at the zoo sitting and sketching whichever wild creatures were caged in front of me.

Getting regular wages again, I resumed my savings habit, keeping back only enough to contribute to household expenses and a small sum for myself, enough to take mother and Doris to the pictures. With my board, together with what Doris was then able to contribute from her wages, our prospects improved considerably.

Another tragedy. Another Christmas.

Before the year was out my poor mother had to endure another tragedy: the death of her husband.

It wasn't such a tragedy to me as I had come to despise my father. He was drinking more than we could afford, and he kept me awake most nights with his alcohol-induced snoring. And Doris, despite her kind and tender nature, wanting so much to love her father, ended up not despising him but blaming him for our misfortunes and our mother's unrelenting melancholy.

Neither of us was home when he passed away; we learned the details only later. It was a hot Wednesday afternoon in December, just before Christmas, nineteen forty-two. Mother said she was ironing in the kitchen when she smelled smoke coming from the lean-to which my father and I still shared as a bedroom. Curious rather than frightened or worried, she went outside, to the lean-to, to find that the bare mattress ticking of my father's bed was smouldering and was about to flare up and set fire to the mattress, the sleeping man lying on it and, indeed, the whole ramshackle lean-to shed, perhaps the whole house. A splash of water from a tin bucket, fetched from the wash-house, was enough to put out the smouldering mattress, but only then did mother realize that her husband was not sleeping but had died, peacefully and painlessly, in his sleep, dropping his lighted cigarette onto the bed in the process.

Mother would have found my father's death unbearable if it weren't for the relief of knowing — from the letters she received regularly from her own mother — that in spite of Hitler's clampdown on circus and show folk, who were all assumed by the Nazis to be Gypsies or Jews, all the members of the world famous Zumpe Human Pyramid were alive and well in Switzerland. Indeed, almost twenty years after her abscondment — she and my father were married in January nineteen twenty-three — her two brothers and two sisters, and two of her girl cousins, had all married circus colleagues and quickly added a new generation of nine young acrobats to the world famous Zumpe troupe.

Once again, then, we — a family of just three — found ourselves facing another Christmas without joy. However, we were invited to share Christmas dinner upstairs with Mr and Mrs Gourley.

They, the always-sad Gourleys, had their own reason to be more glum than usual: their only son, their only child, Eric, was away at war — somewhere in North Africa, they said — and they hadn't heard from him for more than two months. Nevertheless we did our best to enjoy our Christmas dinner; we shared one of mother's chickens, roasted and stuffed, with potatoes and greens from the garden which was now Mr Gourley's alone. It was a quiet affair with each of us trying to be cheerful while having his or her own reason for introspection.

As it turned out, though, my father's death entitled mother to a widow's benefit which, while not generous, was more than the nothing she ever received for her husband's unemployment or illness both of which were due to the same toxic cause. She saw it as a sign that perhaps things were beginning to improve for us. And she was right.

A real job at last.

As I said, I didn't grieve for my father, or miss him at all. Rather, I willingly accepted the role of 'the man of the house'.

I thought it a chiefly financial obligation which led me to an uncharacteristic boldness: I applied for and got a job in a small commercial art studio in Albert Street. My success was due mostly to my drawings of animals and birds done during my breaks at the zoo. The studio was owned by the elderly but somewhat famous 'Bill' Williams who specialized in painting large and flattering oil portraits of Auckland's leading citizens and their race-wining thoroughbreds for an equally large fee. 'Bill' — his real name was Glyn — was a passionate animal lover and so, at the interview, he admired my zoo drawings, ignoring my other work, and gave me the job on the spot.

It was then the end of March, nineteen forty-three, when I was not quite seventeen years old. I quit my zoo job the next day and a week later started work at the studio of 'The Williams Brothers Commercial Art Services Limited' doing sitting-down, clean and easy work, at my own art table, in a tidy studio, next to a window with a fine view along Albert Street, for almost twice the pay I got at the zoo; and for fewer hours.

Although I was technically employed by 'Bill' at the interview I rarely saw the great man. I learned that he was considered a brilliant portrait painter whose mind was 'away with the fairies', a phrase my father used about all writers, poets and painters, and my own artistic ambition. 'Bill' spent most of the day in his own airy loft studio emerging only to have a pipe and share his afternoon tea with his brother Barry and staff.

The business side of the business was cannily managed by his younger brother, the bearded and bow-tied Barry. It was Barry who did the 'commercial' art together with a clever older woman artist called Irma-Leigh Colherne and a white-haired middle-aged bachelor with a bushy white moustache — a Christadelphian — called Morris Johns. An elderly blue-haired bookkeeping lady called Mrs Brady came on Thursdays and Fridays to do the accounts, the banking, pay the wages, and type up and post the brothers' invoices and few letters.

Barry Williams was a kind and gentle man in his mid sixties who treated me like a son. He saw where I sometimes needed guidance with my work but otherwise, when time allowed, in a casual off-hand sort of way, talked about running a small business including how to attract, treat and keep clients, how to run job sheets and keep chargeable hours, how to bill fairly but quickly, to collect debtors and promptly pay creditors and so on. Art-wise, he quickly discovered my aptitude for accurately drawing shoes — for men, women and children — and assigned me the studio's three shoe retailer clients.

While I enjoyed my art work — I secretly thought I had one of the best and most well-paid jobs in the world — I also listened carefully to Barry's business advice guessing the knowledge might one day be useful.

From the lady artist Irma-Leigh I also learned a lot; some about art — she specialized in pastels which I found annoyingly powdery — but more about modern life. Irma-Leigh was especially thin and tall, as tall as me, but her complexion was pale and her head of thick hair was dark red, almost black, and cut brutally short. She smoked constantly — which I assumed made her voice unusually deep— using a long, thin tortoise-shell cigarette holder.

Her attitude to me, as to Morris and her two employers and Mrs Brady, was warm and kind and I appreciated her for treating me as an equal from my first day. She specialized in women's fashions which I thought odd as I saw, at the end of my first day, that under her long and loose-fitting lilac smock Irma-Leigh wore an approximation of men's clothes, from a purple paisley necktie to her taupe trousers and brown-and white-brogues. But I liked her. I liked her detached attitude; how she got on with her work without fuss, and maintained her privacy without seeming aloof, secretive or rude.

Morris, too, was a naturally friendly type who specialized in furniture, sports goods, cycles and motorcycles, cars and trucks. He once tried to give me a Christadelphian leaflet but once rebuffed showed no offence and never did it again. As for old Mrs Brady: I had nothing to do with her, but neither did anyone else. She worked her two days a week in a small cubicle adjacent to the studio's kitchenette. She came out only to go to the post office or bank and, at the end of the day on Thursday, before she went home, to hand out the wage envelopes. Thank you, Mrs Brady, was about the limit of my dealings with the mysterious old woman.

Doris's nurse and the end of the war (almost).
After the shock of my father's sudden death wore off, mother — her grief was brief — admitted later, to

Doris, that she was secretly relieved she no longer had to worry about his drinking and that he would never again, in his drunkenness, force himself on her, leaving her worried and frightened. She never wanted to get pregnant again, confided Doris.

Meanwhile Doris was stepping out with a young man who seemed to be as wan, nervous and shy as Doris herself. His name was Leroy Anderson; he was a nurse in the Americans' Victoria Park hospital, just down the road from us, caring for wounded marines returned from the battle of Guadalcanal.

Doris's affair didn't seem passionate or romantic but Leroy was courteous to mother, and considerate of Doris and her feelings, and so mother approved; Doris seemed happy in a mild sort of way. Leroy made no impression on me. And when, at the end of nineteen forty-four, when the war was almost over and Leroy Anderson was returned to Iowa (or Idaho or Indiana, somewhere starting with 'I'), Doris was unmoved which seemed unnatural even to the unromantic me.

Indeed, except for her brief romance with Private Anderson, Doris — like me — had shown no interest in the progress of the war and when VE day came, at the beginning of May nineteen forty-five, it was acknowledged in Georgina Street only by mother and only with the plain statement: *Gott sei Dank ist Hitler tot.*

The brothers' plan. And my plan.

From my first day with the Williams brothers I worked hard. Which is not to say I found the work hard; on the contrary, I enjoyed everything I did and completed every assignment quickly and easily to the satisfaction of Barry first, then the client, and then with a congratulatory smile from Irma-Leigh and an approving wink and nod from Morris. Furthermore, Barry told me later that most young artists tended to relax with self-indulgent satisfaction after the completion of a large assignment. But you were always keen to get on with the next job, he said. Whatever it was.

Soon, rather than being seen as a shoe specialist, I became known for my versatility. Despite my youth I quickly became favoured by many clients who asked for me to be assigned to their work. That would usually have been discouraged, especially in a bigger studio where artists were kept away from clients, but the Williams brothers were different.

I realized later that they saw in me a rare opportunity. Theirs was a small but well-established studio with a large and loyal client list. But they were getting on in age and evidently saw that this hard working, clever and ambitious young man — me — whom the clients seemed to like and trust, and who had a 'business brain', a rare quality in the creative world, might be persuaded to eventually *buy* their business.

I didn't know about the brothers' plan then. But they didn't know about *my* plans. If they had known they would hardly have believed that anyone so young could be so bold in those uncertain times. But as the war in Europe was over, and the Japanese empire was collapsing, I believed that a fine future was waiting for ambitious young people willing to work hard. I knew that when the Pacific war ended — and surely, I thought, it *must* end soon — more soldiers would come home determined to settle down with their sweethearts, get back to work, buy a house and everything that went with it, and start a family.

Contrary to common opinion, I thought that times were *not* uncertain. I could see that the Williams's business was booming thanks partly to me, my talent, my hard work and, yes, something I had not formerly seen in myself: the ability to get on with clients. It seemed they not only liked my work but actually liked *me* and respected me and my opinions.

I was beginning to believe that one day I really might have my own studio with my own staff, my own clients, and profits that would be all mine.

A new home, car and watch.

At last, at the beginning of August, nineteen forty-five, the war ended with Japan being ruthlessly double atom-bombed by the Americans into a humiliating surrender much to satisfaction of the frightened Pacific nations, large and small, including New Zealand. By then David Purvis, my older cousin, had returned from London and was teaching languages at Auckland's University College. Despite his safe return — which pleased his parents, my uncle and aunt — he and I didn't get on; we never had.

The end of the war also saw the return of the Gourleys' son Eric who came home minus his lower right leg. As a result the Gourleys were given a house in the American army camp at Western Springs which the government had taken over to accommodate returned servicemen and their families. We said goodbye to Mr and Mrs Gourley then and I never saw them or their son again.

Without the Gourleys we would have to pay full rent for the Georgina Street house. Luckily, the city council had lately condemned the house as 'unfit for human habitation' and the government had somehow found us a three-bedroom attached state house in McCulloch Avenue in Three Kings. It was almost new, had a proper wash house and an inside toilet. The luxuriousness of it made mother cry.

I continued to enjoy my work at the Williams's art

studio. The brothers regularly increased my salary, probably aiming to cement my loyalty to the point I couldn't refuse their planned offer. However, I was constantly, consciously and unconsciously, working on my own plans. I continued to save my increasing income having moved my account to the more business-friendly Bank of New Zealand's big Queen Street branch.

I broke into my savings only twice. First to buy a car in order to more easily get to work from Three Kings. It was a well-maintained maroon-and-black nineteen thirty-six Morris 8 two-door. Most days I gave Doris a lift into Karangahape Road although she got the Three Kings tram home, from nearby Symonds Street, as I usually worked later than she did. I was also glad to be able to take mother out for Sunday sight-seeing drives around the city which, I discovered, she hardly knew.

I also bought a silver *Omega* watch to replace my old *Bifora* which by then looked like a lady's watch on my thick and hairy wrist. I might have got a new watch from Uncle Toby's shop but I bought my *Omega* from the big Pascoes store on Queen Street for the full ticketed price; a matter of pride.

Pride was important to me then. I noticed that I was being noticed, which I liked. I wanted to look like a prosperous and sophisticated young man of the world, evidently untroubled by the chaos from which the world was emerging.

And despite the pessimism abroad I really was as full of optimism as my bank account was full of pounds, shillings and pence. I had a nice new home, a car, a new watch, a great job, money in the bank, a happy and contented mother and sister, and the first experience of having a girlfriend.

A wasted summer holiday.

I met Joyce Ronayne — an eighteen-year-old brunette beauty — just before Christmas, nineteen forty-five. She worked at the counter cubicle in a barber shop in Lower Albert Street, taking payment, and thinly veiled suggestive comments, from the men customers as well as selling them, and passing street customers, the cigarettes, tobacco, papers, pipes, pipe cleaners, lighters, razor blades, racing and sports magazines, Australian lottery tickets, and the myriad miscellany of small merchandise which barber shops carried at that time.

I had called in for a haircut and, struck by her beauty when I stopped to pay, I confidently asked her out.

It might seem strange that at almost twenty years old I had no real friends and had never had a girlfriend. Until I met Joyce I had never asked a girl out. I never went to dances and had never even held a girl in my arms let alone kissed one or done anything more or less amorous or intimate.

Looking back I realize that while most blokes my age were preoccupied with girls I was preoccupied with my work; with earning and saving money. And then, suddenly, I was seeing Joyce almost every day. Christmas came but Joyce had to work for most of the three weeks — except the statutory holidays — I was on holiday. The days when the shop was shut, including the weekends, I spent with Joyce at Mission Bay, picnicking, swimming, kissing and cuddling. And then, almost every other day of those holidays, I drove into town to have lunch with her. Usually we sat on a bench beside the ferry buildings, sharing sandwiches, or fish and chips — after which Joyce smoked a cigarette or two — watching the ferries leaving and arriving, belching their black smoke into the clear summer sky.

I was reminded then of the hot holiday days of many summers gone when Willy and I would run down Queen Street or Albert Street, our bare feet burning on the hot pavement, to sneak onto a ferry for a stow-away ride to Devonport. I once told Joyce about my boyhood days with Willy and was disappointed, deflated, when she said that I was being 'silly'. I don't think I would have liked you back then, she said. And, anyway, who cares about them old days when everyone was poor. I hated them days. And Māoris too. I hate Māoris.

You're wasting your holidays on that girl, said mother. I decided, by the time I went back to work, that she was right: I had wasted my precious summer holidays on a girl who might have been a stunning beauty but was also a stunning dummy. It wasn't love but a foolish crush, an infatuation, I admitted to myself. Never again, I thought. Never again.

I returned to work in the middle of January determined to do two things. First, to forget Joyce and my wasted holiday and make the most of what remained of that summer. I made a point of taking mother and Doris to Mission Bay for a picnic every weekend.

My second determination — to make concrete plans for my business future — was pre-empted by my employers who had their own plans.

Mr Bill and Mr Barry want to see you up in Mr Bill's studio, said Mrs Brady on the Thursday afternoon before Easter, nineteen forty-six. Puzzled, and a little suspicious, I made my way up the steep stairs to 'Bill' Williams's studio where I had been interviewed for my job three years earlier.

4

The brothers make an offer.

The brothers' proposal, put to me at an hour-long meeting late that Thursday afternoon before Easter, nineteen forty-six, was simple. I would immediately be included in client meetings and briefings in order to introduce them — the clients — to the idea that they — the brothers — were planning to retire, and that this clever and talented young man — me — was going to take over the business. We'll give it a couple of months to see how it goes, said Barry, but the clients like you and your work already so we're pretty sure they'll be happy.

They also planned to introduce me to the studio's accounts and financial affairs. And finally I would also be introduced to the studio's accountant and lawyer, and encouraged to get my own lawyer for advice. The idea was that I would take over in one year, on my twenty-first birthday, back-dated to the first of April, the beginning of that financial year.

A fixed price was proposed. I thought it was fair although I knew by then that a commercial art studio's only saleable asset was its list of clients, people who are there only because of the service given by the very people who are planning to abandon them. But apparently the brothers believed — or hoped — that their clients would happily transfer their loyalties to me. They could then make a clean exit while I could pay them for the business, in regular instalments, from future profits. On that basis they thought it would take about three years to complete the pay out, less if the business grew and profits exceeded projections.

I promised only to think about it over the long weekend, a promise the brothers accepted. There's no hurry, son, said 'Bill'. The meeting ended with a glass, and then another, of Harvey's Bristol Cream sherry, the brothers' favourite. You give it a good think, said 'Bill', again, as he locked the studio for the weekend.

I did give it 'a good think'.

Their plan was attractive and simple, and evidently sincerely proposed. If I accepted I would quickly become a remarkably young business owner with serious obligations: rented premises, staff and clients, debts, and a three-year repayment commitment. Growth and success would depend entirely on me, my ambition, business skills, hard work and drawing talent. Eventually, three years later but four years from the time of the meeting — which sounded too long to me — and all going well, the business and all its profits, *and problems*, would be mine. And, yes, there was the chance of failure.

On the other hand, my own formative plan — which I had not shared with anyone — was also pretty attractive even in its incompleteness. I would set up a studio, on my own, from scratch. It would be small at first but would be entirely mine. I thought I needed — coincidentally — at least another year. By then I would be twenty-one. I knew that until then it would be impossible to get a business loan or sign a lease. Meanwhile I'd have another year's savings, cash I'd need to fund my way until I had my first client or two. Then

I was sure I would survive in the short term and, in the long term, grow the business. My secret ambition was to have the biggest and best commercial art studio in the city.

Decision made.

I made my decision on the drive home. That done, I had a pleasant and relaxing Easter weekend. I took mother and Doris to the pictures on Saturday night and for a long drive up to Titirangi on the Sunday — my twentieth birthday — where we stopped at a snug little roadside café for Devonshire tea. It was damp and misty high in the Waitakeres; on our way down home it started to rain.

As soon as I got to the studio that Tuesday morning in nineteen forty-six, after the Easter weekend of my twentieth birthday, I told Barry Williams — 'Bill' didn't start until ten o'clock — that I had decided to decline their offer. It's a four year commitment, I said. I was grateful but I didn't want to commit that far ahead.

Barry was gracious. He still treated me more like a son than an employee. I understand, he said kindly, stroking his beard. You're a young man, Eddie. Got your whole life ahead of you. I do understand. And so will Bill. We just hope you stay around for a while yet.

I did stay with the studio. For nearly three years.

'Bill' Williams died a year later. He was seventy-two years old. Although he was mourned by the Auckland business and political classes, for his portrait painting of thoroughbred horses and their human owners, he must now be faded out of my story.

His death didn't affect the commercial art side of the business under Barry's management. I continued to be in demand by the studio's clients and so continued to earn well and save money. I needed a new car, and could easily have afforded something more modern and reliable than my Morris 8, but I put up with it for the sake of my bank account.

Mother complains; Doris has a new boyfriend.

Mother's health improved in Mount Roskill. She was immensely relieved that her years of hardship and poverty were over and would probably never return. Sometimes she worried about me and said things like: Oh, Eddie, you are too ambitious; or, I think you work too hard, Eddie; or You're getting greedy and you care too much about money. But even as she spoke she must have known I wouldn't change.

Doris had a new boyfriend. He was a few years older than her and somewhat strange. I remember his name was Harry Burrell. Evidently he had once qualified as an accountant, and if pressed could talk business, but he'd never practised and was now studying for the priesthood at Saint John's College. Doris as the wife of a priest would be very nice, said mother. But I had doubts. I thought he just needed a girl's company for dances and socials. Nevertheless Doris seemed to be fond of Harry and went to church with him on Sundays; to the old cathedral in Parnell.

My own art studio.

On the Friday before Labour weekend, nineteen forty-eight, I told Barry about my plans to go out on my own. I told him I'd finish at Christmas if that was all right with him. Barry accepted my resignation in advance; he seemed to be expecting it.

And so, at the beginning of January, nineteen forty-nine, while the rest of New Zealand was on holiday, I was setting up my one-room studio in the Dilworth building. It wasn't ideal — tiny, with just a single window — but it was located well for business, and it was affordable. It was part of a suite overseen by an attractive and efficient lady who answered the phone, took messages, typed letters and accounts, delivered and collected mail, and undertook a variety of other secretarial services and errands for 'her' dentist, herbalist and tailor as well as the new tenant, the young Eddie Purvis, commercial artist.

At that time, early in January, I was the only occupant of the shared suite; the dentist, herbalist, tailor and secretary — I had met them only once — were all on holiday. It seemed that the whole great concrete building, usually busy with people coming and going, footfalls in the halls, doorbells buzzing and telephones jangling — in which I had just one small room — was altogether empty.

My first client.

So I was surprised one morning when I heard a faint, hesitant knock on the door of the suite's ante-room; someone was in the unlit corridor trying to attract attention. Are you Mr Purvis? asked a lovely and smiling young lady standing in the corridor, a stylish bag over her right padded shoulder, a practical satchel under her other arm. She was beautiful and fashionable and reminded me of Rita Hayworth. Eddie, I insisted. Call me Eddie. Come in, come in, I said enthusiastically as I steered her across the empty ante-room into the single room which was my new studio.

Barbara Ormeskirke — call me Barbara, she said — was a junior copywriter in the advertising department of Milne & Choyce, a Queen Street department store. She had been sent by her manager to find 'that artist who used to do so much work for John Court', a rival department store. We couldn't use you when you were with the Williams brothers, she said, but now... Now you can, I announced with a flourish. But I couldn't find you, said Barbara, I had to ring up Mr Barry. He told me where to find you. Did he mind you ringing up? I asked. I don't think so, said Barbara. He was very nice actually.

So what can I do for Milnes? I asked, working hard to suppress my excitement. My first client already; a big department store. Well, we're working on our Easter sale, she said. It's going to be really big this year and we need your help. Mr Hines said there's no one like you for hats — ladies' and men's — and shoes.

And with that Purvis Commercial Art had its first client.

Such a glamorous girlfriend.

I had a brief romance with the beautiful and glamorous Barbara Ormeskirke. We went dancing at the Peter Pan or the Wintergarden a few times, on Saturday nights, and to the pictures during the week. I even took her home to meet mother and Doris.

Mother approved — and said so — but Doris said she wore flashy clothes. But she works in a big fashionable department store, I protested. And she wears too much make-up, Doris added. Ditto, I said. And she likes the good life and is too ambitious for a woman, continued Doris although I don't know how she knew such things about poor Barbara. It's just not seemly, she said.

I didn't say it then but Doris's objections were the very things I liked about Barbara. In the end, though, it didn't matter as three months later Barbara was on a ship to England. What happened to her there, and whether she ever came back to New Zealand, I never knew, and so she fades out of my story.

New advertising clients.

The Milnes business grew despite Barbara Ormeskirke's departure. I got on well not only with her replacement but also with Alec Hines, the store's advertising manager. Milnes had their own artists but they used me for big events and sales. Before long I was working late most nights, often on weekends, to keep up with their work.

And thanks to Milne & Choyce's newspaper advertising, I began to get work from some of the city's biggest advertising agencies which were growing fast as the country recovered from the war. However, attractive as the advertising assignments were, I found it hard to keep up. My bank balance was growing quickly but I knew it couldn't last. If the business kept growing I'd have to get staff and find bigger premises.

New government.

Nineteen forty-nine ended with the election of the first National government. After fourteen years of Labour the people were tired of shortages and restrictions and saw the National Party's promise of a new era of prosperity and freedom to be the answer for the second half of the century.

Like most young and ambitious men of my generation I thought the National government's policies would be good for my small but thriving business. You see, by then I thought of myself not as an artist but as a businessman who happened to be in the *business* of commercial art.

My old boss.

Late the next year Barry Williams asked for a meeting. We met at the Northern Club, where Barry was a member, on the Friday evening before Labour weekend, two years since the day I resigned from Barry's studio. After shaking hands, with genuine manly affection as I recall, in the portico of the historic stone clubhouse in Princes Street, sitting down in the bar and getting courtesies out of the way, Barry explained the awful reason for the meeting.

Martha is dying, he said. Cancer. I *have* to retire. I have no choice. But the studio? At that point I saw tears in the old man's eyes. He, Barry, looked embarrassed and quickly wiped them away with the back of his hands. I've tried to sell it, he said. Offered it to you of course. I squirmed a little at that but said nothing. Barry continued: Don't worry, son. I understand. But since Bill died I've tried everything but, well, there's just no buyers. As you know yourself, it's easy to start up on your own these days. I don't really care for myself. I don't need the money. I can pay everyone and close up shop with a clear conscience. But I'm worried about Irma-Leigh and Morris. Mrs Brady's not a problem. She wants to retire anyway.

I interrupted: But Irma-Leigh and Morris are good artists, I said. They'll get jobs easily. They're both getting on, I'm afraid, said Barry with a slow head shake. It's the fifties now, Eddie. A young person's world.

My old colleagues become my new staff.
At that moment I knew what was being asked and I consciously took the inevitable step. I can use them, I said emphatically at which moment I saw Barry Williams's face relax and, again, wetness come to his eyes. I was hoping, said Barry, but I didn't dare. I mean, you're the talk of the town, son. Your success, I mean.

I've got too much work, I said. They'll be terrific. But I can't do anything until I get new premises. You should see the cupboard I work in. So, yes, tell them as soon as

I get new premises. What about their salaries, Eddie? Can you afford their salaries? They'll generate their own salaries, I said. And some. You taught me that, Barry. I did, didn't I, said Barry with a smile.

New premises.

Martha Williams, Barry's sick wife, died almost a year later by which time Purvis Commercial Art was established in an historic two-storied brick house — one of three in a terrace — in Symonds Street. Now, not only were Irma-Leigh Colherne and the Christadelphian Morris John working for me, kept busy partly by the accounts they brought with them — Barry Williams had had no objection — but I had also employed another young artist. He soon moved on but was replaced by a series of clever and ambitious young artists whose names I can't remember but who reminded me of myself. I also had a pretty young receptionist/secretary called Glenda, fresh out of secretarial college.

Barry Williams, overcome with grief, in failing health himself, moved to New Plymouth to live with his daughter and son-in-law. Accordingly, he too must be faded out of my story.

A waterfront strike makes the National government stronger.

For the greater part of that year — nineteen fifty-one — New Zealand was rattled by a strike of militant waterfront workers. It would have crippled the economy if not for government intervention and the deployment of the army to load vital exports.

Purvis Commercial Art was largely untouched by the widespread agitation and violence. Only once, one Friday at the beginning of June, was I exposed to the union's anger when I was stopped from crossing Queen

Street, to visit Milnes, due to a protest which had turned ugly. I was reminded then of that long-ago day — I was only six years old — when my father came home from another Queen Street riot with torn clothes, a black eye, and a battery-operated portable radio which mother refused to have in the house.

Anyway, the Waterfront Workers' Union didn't have any public support and eventually, in July, was forced to admit defeat. The government took advantage of the public's anger and resentment by calling a snap election which resulted in an increased majority for the National party. It was a result which delighted me; more than ever I was benefitting from the country's booming economy.

The price of success.

By the next year, though, I was disillusioned. Purvis Commercial Art continued to attract new accounts which kept me and my three artists busy, frequently working nights and weekends. My staff were well paid and would not normally mind working late or weekends *occasionally*. But the volume of work became so great that working overtime became 'normal' and I was obliged to pay overtime rates which cut into my profits.

You're too busy with your work, complained mother. Doris and me, we never see you. You've got a lovely new car — I'd bought a near-new Zephyr Six — but you never take us out anymore. You've changed and I don't like it.

I didn't like it either. I didn't like letting down mother but I couldn't explain my dilemma to her. She had no experience of business; no understanding of the pressures I was under; how I felt responsible for my staff and how I just *couldn't* slacken off and let down my clients.

Doris, at twenty-eight years old, was spending all her

leisure time at home. Harry Burrell, her one-time priestly boyfriend, had long left the scene to be replaced by no one. She still worked at McKenzie's and was — I thought — destined for a sad and lonely spinsterhood. I felt sorry for her. In my work I met and mixed with the city's most attractive, fashionable, glamorous and confident young women. Compared with them Doris looked merely glum, plain and dowdy. But there was nothing I could do to help her. Nothing. And, anyway, she didn't seem to care.

I had a worrisome Christmas/summer holiday that year. I managed to have Christmas dinner at home with mother and Doris, and, in the afternoon, to take them to visit Uncle Toby and Aunt Edith where I was surprised to find that my aloof cousin David had a new and equally snotty wife. But I spent each day after Christmas, including weekends, at the studio catching up with work that hadn't been finished before the holidays.

By the time the staff returned in the middle of January, happy, refreshed, and wanting to share their holiday stories, I felt mentally and physically exhausted and pessimistic. The success I had wanted and worked for was now a burden I couldn't unload; I felt trapped.

And then someone surprising turned my pessimism into enthusiastic optimism.

A lesson in advertising.

It happened late one hot Friday afternoon at the end of January. I was sitting at my table, a window open behind me letting in a refreshing breeze, relaxing with a bottle of beer. Irma-Leigh Colherne stopped on her way out. A word? she asked. I nodded and waited as she drew a chair from the adjacent table, sat down, crossed her elegantly trousered legs, and lit a cigarette in her long, thin tortoise-shell cigarette holder.

I must say you look like shit gone cold, she said. I was surprised. I'd never heard Irma-Leigh swear before; rarely heard *any* woman swear. I smiled and shrugged. Come on, Eddie, she said. You've got it all wrong. Got what wrong? I asked as I took a drink. *Tout!* she said. Eh? I was genuinely puzzled.

Look, Eddie, she continued, you're only a kid. How old are you anyway? Nearly twenty-seven, I replied. Well, you're a *wunderkind*. You know the word? I know *some* German, I fudged. Well, then, said the woman who was more than twice my age, you know my meaning. Twenty-seven, got your own business, staff, including *moi*, nice car, plenty of *moolah*, big success, but full of worries, right? No free time. No fun. No girlfriend. No nookie. I raised my eyebrows at that and nodded slowly in resigned agreement. So, continued Irma-Leigh, if you're not careful you're going to have a breakdown or something. She took a drag on her cigarette and I took a drink.

Ever heard of Charles Barker? she asked. I shook my head. I didn't know who she was talking about. Well, she continued, Charles Barker isn't a person but a bloody big advertising agency in *Londinium* town. Fact is, it's the oldest advertising agency in the whole bloody world.

I must have looked puzzled. I took another drink while my companion drew heavily on her cigarette. Thing is, she said, I used to work there. For years in fact. Only came back here cause I got up the duff with Nigel.

I knew nothing of about Irma-Leigh's private life. So what are you saying? I asked, intrigued. Look, she said, I know how things work. What things? I asked. Well, look, *par exemple*: I just finished those wash drawings of all those new Clarks shoes for Cassrels Advertising, right, the new winter range. You give them to the agency, charge them a one-off fee, they pay you, you pay me, end of story, right? But wrong. Firstly, the agency plusses up your invoice. Ten, twenty per cent. Maybe more these days, I don't know. Then they put the shoes in an ad, add a headline, some crappy copy, a logo, charge the client for all that, and get paid. But then comes the *real* money. They put the ad in papers all over the country. Could run for weeks. Months. Some ads run the same for years. And the agency gets a commission, twenty per cent sometimes, every time the ad appears anywhere. Every time. For doing absolutely nothing.

I sat up straight at that, refilled my glass, and said: You're right. Course I'm right, Eddie lad. I'll see you Monday. And she was gone leaving her cigarette smoke hanging in the warm air.

Money for nothing.

I then discovered that many of my smaller clients, who managed their own advertising, were happy to hand over the whole messy business to me. And so, hardly without trying, Purvis Commercial Art became a *de facto* advertising agency. I was still too busy, still working nights and weekends, still receiving complaints from mother, but I was banking more money than ever, every month, from the commissions — 'money for nothing' I called it — on all the newspaper and magazine advertising I placed for my clients.

From art studio to (unaccredited) advertising agency.

I had a lot to learn about the advertising business but I was a quick learner when it came to money. I frequently took advice from Irma-Leigh including sending away for Otto Kleppner's famous book. It's the bloody bible, she said. I kept it on my desk for years, and referred to it frequently.

I soon learned that not any business could become an advertising agent and get repeat advertising commissions. Until I could prove our credit-worthiness I could place advertising only through a fully accredited agency which would pass on only half of the commissions received, keeping the other half as compensation for their willingness to take a risk with a tyro business.

Introducing Terry Staines and Tom Wolfendale.

I also learned that while Irma-Leigh and old Morris John were familiar with the process of creating complete advertisements, beyond the illustrations, they were unskilled with the scheduling and placing of advertising in national and local newspapers and magazines. That was a discipline more like bookkeeping. So I employed an experienced media manager, a somewhat dour middle-aged man known in the business for his meticulous attention to detail. His name was Terry Staines.

You're bloody lucky to get Terry, said Irma-Leigh.

At first I felt odd employing a man so much my senior who looked and acted more like a professional — a doctor, perhaps, or a lawyer or accountant — than an employee of a young and small advertising agency. Fact is, old man, said Terry later, I was jolly glad to get out of that place. He was referring to his previous employer. So stuffy, he said. I liked the idea of being in a small outfit on the move.

Terry urged me to replace the old sole-practitioner accountant recommended by Uncle Toby. You need someone young, your own age, said Terry. Someone with the same ideas as you, the same ambition. I appointed the new firm which had just moved into the house/office at the other end of the Symonds Street terrace. It was led by the dynamic young Tom Wolfendale, my age, who proved to be a clever accountant, a wise business counsellor, and a good friend.

By then I had a list of loyal clients who always paid on time which meant I was always on time paying Charles Haines, the agency which placed my advertising and shared my commissions. And so, in just eighteen months — that is, in the middle of nineteen fifty-four — Purvis Commercial Art was granted full accreditation.

Good on you, Eddie, said the Charles Haines media manager — old, crusty but kindly disposed to the young me — over a cup of tea in the big agency's canteen. You'll do well. Thanks, I said hardly believing I would no longer have to share my commissions. But one thing, added the older man. What's that? I asked impatiently; I wanted to get away and share the news with Terry and the others. Change your name, he said. Purvis Advertising or something. Whatever you like, but put 'advertising' in your name.

The next couple of years passed smoothly for the agency which I renamed and, with Tom Wolfendale's help, formed into a company: Purvis Advertising Limited. I was the only shareholder except for a small share held in mother's name. Growth was steady and the professional help of Irma-Leigh Colherne (with her Charles Barker experience), Terry Staines (running the media buying) and Tom Wolfendale (looking after the financials) meant I was able to reclaim a personal life and some leisure time.

Changes at home.
It was only then — spending evenings and weekends at

home — I noticed that mother, always so active, fit and lissom, had put on weight and become slow and somewhat despondent. She was not yet fifty and yet she looked and acted years older.

I mentioned it to Doris who was indignant. You've just noticed *now?* she protested. You're so busy with your stupid business, Eddie. But what is it, Dossy? I asked. She got a letter that her father died, said Doris. Our grandfather. A couple of months ago.

Mama, I didn't know, I said to mother who surrendered her now somewhat soft and round body to my embrace. He was an old man, she said. Just more than seventy-five years old. But it still hurts. I didn't see him for more than thirty years. And your mother? I asked. Your *Oma*, said mother. She is old too, but quite well she says. We write often. She broke away then to fetch an old framed and faded photo of her young parents from the kitchen dresser. I was a terrible *Tochter*, Eddie, to leave them like that, she said. She showed me the photo; I had seen it every day of my life but had never studied it closely. There, said mother. So beautiful, yes? But will I see her again? I don't know. I don't think so.

I promised myself then to pay more attention to mother's needs. One day, I thought, I might be able to send her to Germany to see her mother and family. Perhaps. If the agency keeps doing well.

The agency did do well but mother never saw her family or her homeland again.

I noticed that Doris too had changed. No longer shy and shrinking, she seemed to be suddenly independent and assertive. She told me she had been promoted to store manager at McKenzie's. She'd also bought an economical little car: a grey Morris Minor, almost new. I was impressed. At that time very few women were licensed to drive a motor car; they were thought by men to lack the necessary mechanical 'sense'. Now *she* could take mother shopping and on weekend outings for which I no longer had time. Good on you, Dossy, I said although a look from the no longer meek and mild-mannered Doris told me I was being patronizing.

Finally, at the end of nineteen fifty-five, when I was confident that the agency's success was real and sustainable, and would undoubtedly continue to deliver large profits, I proposed buying our own house. But mother had no desire to move from the state house she was granted after the war; Doris too said she was perfectly happy in McCulloch Avenue. I decided it was time to get a place of my own.

I know where I'm going, I said. It'll be a birthday present to myself.

A stranger in the office.

On the day before my thirtieth birthday I waited anxiously for the Barfoot and Thompson land agent to pick me up for the drive out to Mission Bay; I was to view a flat there. But Glenda told me a stranger was asking for me in reception. Not the land agent, she said. It's a Mr Brown, Bill Brown.

It's Willy, said the apparent stranger. Willy Parāone. You must remember. I was shocked. Without being told I wouldn't have recognized my childhood friend, the scruffy little barefoot Māori kid from Elizabeth Street, now dressed in a navy-blue suit, white shirt, burgundy tie (with a gold tie-clip) and shiny brown shoes. But... I stuttered, but Willy held up his hands to stop me. I know, I know, he said. I wouldn't have recognized you either, you rich old bastard. All suited and tied, with a spiffy little Clark Gable moustache and a flash watch. I looked down at my new *Rolex*, somehow pleased that

Willy had noticed it.

At last we crossed the room, smiling, almost laughing. We met in the middle and began shaking hands vigorously. Neither of us knew what to ask, say or do next until I pointed across the room to Glenda. But Glenda said Mr Brown, I said. Mr Bill Brown. I know, I know, said Willy quickly. It's a long story. Well come and tell me, I said. In my office. Come on. And then, turning to Glenda, I said: No calls, eh. Nothing. Glenda smiled and nodded understandingly, but quickly asked: What about the Barfoot man?

But I ignored her. I wanted to talk to Willy.

5

Willy's story.

Willy's story *was* a long one which he began in my office and continued and ended over lunch — a hot sausage roll and a cup of tea — in The Lunch Box, a favourite little lunch bar a few doors up from the agency. In short though it amounted to this: when he was eleven Willy's mother and his older brother decided he was not Māori enough so he was sent to stay with whānau on a small marae in Dargaville. Actually I knew all that and easily remembered the day Willy left.

Once up north he quickly got fluent in Māori which pleased the auntie — his father's sister — who had been charged with his education. Later he was sent to stay with another auntie, in the town, where he attended Dargaville High School with his cousins. Got my school cert there, bloody prefect, everything, eh, he said.

From there he went to Whangarei where he started work in the accounts office at Wright-Stephenson before being promoted to sales where he proved to be a natural salesman. Got on real good with the cockies, he said. And their wives, he added with a typical Willy wink.

But your name? I asked. Willy said that his Māori name was 'a bit of a handicap' in Pākehā circles up north. My boss suggested I change it. Said it would make things easier. Parāone is just Māori for Brown, he said. And Willy sounds like a kid's name — my real name's Wiremu for William — so I changed it to Bill. Do I have to call you Bill now? I asked. If you don't mind, mate, he said. If you don't mind.

So what are you doing in Auckland? I asked. Willy said his father had died. Never recovered from the war, eh, he said. His mother wanted to move back to Dargaville and he and his brother had to help her shift, sell the Elizabeth Street house and all the furniture. All done now, he said, but it took a while. Now I'm going back. But first I had to catch up with my rich old delinquent mate Eddie. And here I am.

Listen, I said. I'm having a birthday party tomorrow. My thirtieth. You've gotta come, Willy. I mean Bill. Meet everybody. Can't, mate, said Willy with a slow shake of his head. Sorry, Eddie, but I'm going straight back up north now. Be back here next month though. Catch up then, eh.

Bill Brown, account executive.

A month later Bill Brown was back in Auckland, staying with a cousin in Surrey Crescent. And a month after that he was learning — from me and others — the work of an advertising account executive. It was a job to which the tall, dark, handsome, intelligent and hugely charming Bill Brown was ideally suited. Before long he had his own client list, his own secretary, and was making a disproportionately high contribution to Purvis Advertising's continued growth.

Out of the office Bill and I resumed our childhood friendship. In fact it wasn't until Bill arrived I realized I had no real friends. And Bill was so self-assured — so confident — that it never occurred to him to be anything but my old mate. He was getting a good salary and he liked his independence; after years of crowded living with whānau he was happy to live alone in a small flat in Grafton.

A bigger studio. And a new home.

Sometimes I couldn't believe the exceedingly profitable growth of my once little art studio. There was a growth in staff numbers too which meant the charming little Victorian two-storied terrace house on Symonds Street became too small. Conveniently, though, the middle house of the terrace — between the agency and Wolfendale Mills, Accountants — became vacant and was taken over by Purvis Advertising Limited at the beginning of the next financial year.

Confident of my financial security, I leased a flat in the posh and expensive Garden Court Apartments on the beach at Mission Bay. By then Doris was living above a shop in Karangahape Road, close to her work, with her friend Ngaire. Mother was therefore left alone in McCulloch Avenue. She said she didn't mind. She had a man friend then; a Dutch immigrant called Franz Vanderloos. Anyway, before I moved out I bought her a new lounge suite, fridge and washing machine. She liked that.

Introducing Lily.

Bill's friendship brought many changes to my life including a wife.

Bill was sociable; he loved parties and dances and seemed to know most of the city's dance bands. And he could sing. Used to sing with all the bands up north, he said. At dances he was often invited on stage to sing.

By nineteen fifty-seven rock-and-roll was beginning to dominate the hit parade and although Bill could sing all the popular songs of the day neither of us — at thirty years old — cared for jiving. Instead we sought the more conservative and traditional dances where we could hold a girl in our arms and fox-trot, quick-step and waltz the night away, finishing with a tasty supper, a cup of tea, and perhaps a pretty girl to take home. It was at the traditional Saturday night dance at the Point Chevalier Sailing Club I met Lily and Bill met Penny.

They say truth is stranger than fiction and it definitely was in our case. Bill and I were friends. Lily and Penny were friends; they were both a couple of years younger than us. They were both teachers: Lily at Point Chevalier Primary and Penny at Pasadena Intermediate. Like us, they'd been childhood friends; they'd grown up in the same street in Point Chevalier — Johnstone Street — just a short walk from the sailing club. After the dance on that fateful Saturday night, rather than Bill and I going our separate ways, each driving a girl home, we left our cars in Harbour View Road and walked the girls home together; a real foursome.

Then, eighteen months later — in January nineteen fifty-eight, the Saturday of Anniversary Weekend — there was a double wedding at the Church of the Ascension in Dignan Street where Lillian Braithwaite became Lily Purvis and Penelope Lamont became Penny Parāone.

Minehaha Avenue. And introducing John.
Late the previous year — nineteen fifty-seven — the newly-elected Labour government had introduced what was known as the 'black budget' which included big tax increases on beer and cigarettes, widely considered to be the simple, harmless and affordable pleasures of the working-class supporters of the Labour party. Unsurprisingly, the Labour government survived only

one term and — much to my relief — was replaced in November nineteen sixty by the National government led by Keith Holyoake.

By then Lily and I were living in a sprawling nineteen thirties Californian bungalow on a huge double section in Minehaha Avenue in Takapuna. The Auckland Harbour Bridge had been opened in May the previous year and, believing that the Labour government couldn't last, that business and public morale would improve once it was gone, and that the population and popularity of the North Shore would both boom once the bridge was open, Bill and I invested heavily in North Shore property.

As well as the house in Takapuna I bought a large tract of ex-farmland in then rural Brown's Bay — where I remembered camping one long-ago summer — while Bill bought a two-storied Victorian kauri mansion in Narrow Neck and two orchards in rural Rosedale.

Lily had stopped teaching by the time we moved to Minehaha; three months later, on Boxing Day, nineteen sixty, John Maxwell Purvis was born.

New premises. And a new name.

My bank account was awash with money then and I was looking to invest in commercial property. At the same time, Tom Wolfendale's accounting firm, Wolfendale Mills, tenant of the house at the other end of the Symonds Street terrace, was looking for new premises. And so, together, we — Tom Wolfendale and I — bought a new three-storied office block, with basement parking, in Parnell Road. Wolfendale Mills took the ground floor while the newly-named Purvis/Brown agency occupied the top two floors with access to the roof garden.

By then I was a truly wealthy man. And so, to a lesser

extent, was my friend Bill Brown. I gave him a small shareholding and made him a director of the agency. Renamed Purvis/Brown Advertising and Marketing Limited, it bore no resemblance to the little one-man one-room art studio I had opened in the Dilworth building in January nineteen forty-nine.

Indeed, the only links to a time even before the agency's beginnings — the artists Irma-Leigh Colherne and Morris John — had both retired and so must be faded out of my story. I was sad to see them go. They had, at the beginning, given me the advertising experience I lacked. But I also knew they belonged in the past; to an advertising world that no longer existed. Photography had largely replaced illustrations in print advertising. We were also doing a lot of radio and our highly creative and respected radio department was always busy.

The coming of television.

I knew that television — and television advertising — would present new opportunities. While most of my big competitors were complacent about television I knew that television advertising was inevitable.

In nineteen sixty-two, with an eye on the future and ahead of most of even my biggest competitors — even well ahead of demand — I began to prepare for television. Television advertising was booming in Australia, where commercial television had been broadcasting since nineteen fifty-six. Capitalizing on a friendship made, at a Wellington media conference, with Terry O'Connor, the managing director of a Sydney agency, I spent what Tom Wolfendale considered a 'small fortune' on what he also called 'a waste of time' — It'll never happen, he said — on my first international aeroplane flight: an almost six-hour journey on a TEAL

Douglas DC-6 from Whenuapai airport to Sydney's Kingsford-Smith.

There, in Sydney, I spent a week with my friend's television department which specialized in retail advertising for Mark Foy's, one of Sydney's biggest department stores. After a week, staying at the luxurious Menzies hotel, I considered myself knowledgeable enough to talk sensibly about television advertising and to advise on its creation, production and scheduling.

I was only thirty-six then and yet I felt old, wise and experienced. Indeed, on the drive home, over the bridge, at the end of the day, I often wondered at my own success. How did it all happen? What did I do to deserve so much success? I had a hugely successful business, great staff, a fabulous car — I had recently bought a new EK Holden — land in Brown's Bay, plenty of investments, money in the bank, a wonderful house in Takapuna's best street, a beautiful wife, a little baby boy and another baby on the way. I decided I had every reason to be pleased with myself. And proud.

Goodbye, Uncle Toby.

At the end of one such end-of-day drive, in July nineteen sixty-two, I arrived home to learn from the very pregnant Lily that my Uncle Toby had died suddenly. Your mother rang up. When? About half an hour ago, said Lily. It's just happened and she's terribly upset. You'll have to go over and see her. Lily was right. Mother was terribly upset. Doris (and Ngaire) were already there, at McCulloch Avenue, doing their best to comfort her. But when I arrived she fell immediately into my embrace. Poor Toby, she said. Such a good man, *der Bruder deines Vaters,* your father's brother. Such a good man to us all this time. And now he is gone.

After a lifetime in the jewellery business Uncle Toby

had sold his Queen Street shop and was looking forward to a comfortable retirement with my Aunt Edith. I had only fond memories of him; memories mixed with gratitude for all he had done for mother as well as for me, child, adolescent and man.

The funeral, at Saint Aiden's in Remuera, was especially crowded; Tobias Purvis was highly respected by the Auckland business community. I spoke there of his business and community achievements and, speaking for mother, of his generosity and many great kindnesses to my small family.

Mother grieved again, later, when she learned that her sister-in-law Edith, Toby's wife, my aunt, was moving to Wellington to be with her son David. She's the last link to your father, she said sadly. And I'll probably never see her again. And she never did.

Introducing Lisa.

Lily was painfully, heavily pregnant at Toby's funeral; she had to sit for the whole service. A little more than a week later, on the twenty-eighth of July, at the little North Shore maternity hospital, she gave birth to a healthy little girl we called Lisa Marie.

John — who was eighteen months old then — had been delivered quickly and easily but Lily laboured for many exhausting hours before little Lisa was born. The next day, tired and sore, Lily insisted: No more, she said. I'm never going through that again. I was puzzled. What do you mean? I asked. I'm going on that new pill thing as soon as I get out of here, she said. As a result my family was limited to the 'ideal' of one boy and one girl.

A shocking confession.

Something about Lisa's birth and Lily's contraceptive pill announcement caused Lily's mother to make a shocking confession. Lily was in the hospital with Lisa for more than a week; she received her mother's confession almost as soon as she got home. I learned about it only that night.

I thought about it for a few days before confiding in Bill. We were in my office sharing an end-of-day beer. Most of the staff had left so the agency was dark and eerily quiet. Outside it was August cold; a strong wind was pitching rain rattlingly against the office windows. The thing is, I said to Bill, you knew Lily's older sister, right? Grace? Yeah, I remember her, said Bill. Much older. That's her, I said. Fifteen years older than Lily. And never married. Still lives at home with her mother.

We poured more beer and took a drink before I continued. The thing is, I said, Lily's just found out that Grace isn't actually her older sister. Eh? Bill was puzzled. Mate, I said, you ready for this? Go on, said Bill. The thing is, I said, Grace is Lily's *mother*. Her *real* mother. Bill was astonished. What?

I had to explain to Bill what Lily had explained to me what her mother — actually her grandmother — had explained to her: that Grace had been a difficult and rebellious child, had run away from home when she was just fourteen and had come home a few months later pregnant with Lily. She gave birth just after her fifteenth birthday. Poor Lil, said Bill. What does she think of that? She doesn't know what to think, I said. And neither do I. She now knows who her real mother is but has no idea about her father. He'd be John and Lisa's grandfather, I said with a puzzled shrug.

Lily's (grand)mother must have sensed something — a premonition perhaps, said Lily — that made her confess her guilty secret after thirty-two years. Because she died, suddenly, before the year was out, ten years after her husband, leaving everything to Grace, her only child and Lily's *real* mother. The saddest thing then, for everyone concerned, was to see that as hard as Grace and Lily tried to act as mother and daughter it was impossible; their relationship never recovered.

Lily: a natural mother.

Lily was a natural and loving mother who devoted the next few years to the children. Despite admitting that she longed to go back to teaching she happily applied herself to the routine duties of a housewife and even more happily to the health, welfare and education of John and Lisa. As a mother she seemed to know that being home with the children was important, especially as I was rarely home for long. She also openly hugged and cuddled the children a lot which actually made me a bit uncomfortable. I couldn't do it. And she said it was important to talk and listen and answer all their questions. You have to, she said. Every single thing children see for the first time is new and mysterious.

How do you know all this stuff? I asked her once. Parenting was a mystery to me. I don't know, she said. I just do, that's all.

Lily did her best to include Grace — her newly-revealed mother, the children's grandmother — in the children's lives. But as much as she tried Lily couldn't bring herself to see Grace as anything but a somewhat surly older sister while Grace seemed unable to 'be' a grandmother. I think she's jealous about the children, Lily said once. Not married and never will be. But she had *you*, I said. Obviously different, said Lily. She acts weird. I much preferred it when she was my stupid big sister. And, anyway, there should be a grandfather. Thank God for *your* mother though, she added. A *proper* lovely grandmother.

My mother — whose affair with the Dutchman didn't

last — *was* the perfect grandmother; babysitting the children when they were babies, and spoiling them with unlimited and non-judgemental grandmotherly love as they grew, insisting — against my wishes — that they call her *Oma,* and rewarding them, for their very existence, with the sort of extravagant gifts she never could afford for me and Doris.

The love she lavished on young John and Lisa only increased when she learned from Germany that her eighty-year-old mother had died. In her sleep. No pain, she said. Is how we all should go. I only wish. Mother was not quite sixty then but she looked and seemed much older.

Home versus work.

I loved my children but, to be honest, looking back, probably not enough. Like many men, I suppose, I was preoccupied with my work which in my case was not merely a job but a business I owned; a business that continued to grow and be exceedingly profitable.

But despite the satisfaction I got from my success I was also burdened with the responsibility I felt for my employees and their families. I knew that if the agency failed then forty-plus people — actually I can't remember the exact number then — would be out of work. The thought of failure made me grimace involuntarily. As a result I stayed in my office most nights, long after everyone had left, torn between whatever I was doing there and getting home in time to have tea with Lily and the children. I liked to help bathe them and get them into bed; perhaps take my turn to read them a story as they dropped off to sleep. I liked it when that happened but, to be honest, I did little to ensure that it did.

They do love it when you're home at night, said Lily.

I wish you could do it more. I know, I said. If only. But somehow the end-of-day pull of the office was stronger than the pull of wife, children and home.

Lily and Playcentre.

When the Takapuna Playcentre opened, in September, nineteen sixty-five, Lily was one of the first mother volunteers; and John — who was to start school in the new year — and Lisa were amongst the first to be enrolled.

Playcentre was a parents-organized and -run pre-school where Lily, as an experienced primary school teacher, was welcomed. It was there she suddenly made more friends than she had since moving to Takapuna. She had a little red Austin Mini then so she was suddenly independent and mobile, buzzing around the North Shore, shopping and taking the children here, there and everywhere as young mothers did and do.

Over the next few years — until Lisa started school — Lily spent many volunteer hours and days working mostly with other mothers but sometimes with fathers who had volunteered to do garden and building maintenance. I wish you'd come along, she often said. Lots of dads are there. You'd enjoy it. But I was rarely able to spare a Saturday morning; and when I did I didn't enjoy it although I pretended I did for Lily's sake. Inevitably, though, as soon as the men's Saturday morning working bee was over I'd head back to the office to catch up with whatever needed catching up with which sometimes was nothing.

When John started school at the beginning of nineteen sixty-six Lily said she felt freer than she had felt since he was born. She still had Lisa to care for but she was more engaged than ever with Playcentre — she was on the committee — and had joined a ladies' badminton club where she made even more friends. And with the increased freedom, relieved of the worries of mothering children through infancy, it seemed to dawn on Lily — perhaps for the first time — that she was married to a successful young man, approaching forty, who was somewhat notorious in the advertising industry. And was rich.

Lily and money.

She also discovered — she told me later — that none of her friends had a personal bank account, as she did, into which her husband deposited a large monthly allowance. She found she had money which, she knew, she could never spend not only because it was such a large amount but also because she'd always been careful with money.

She knew a little of my poor childhood — a drunken father and a worried and unhappy mother — and attributed my ambition and success to a determination to never again be poor. She, on the other hand, had enjoyed a comfortable childhood in which her Baptist father — actually her grandfather — worked hard to provide for his family while her mother — actually her grandmother — instilled a respect for hard-earned money and a contempt for extravagance and waste.

Suddenly, as my fortieth birthday approached, I sensed that Lily — now less occupied with the children — was beginning to resent the business that kept me so busy; more absent than present in family life. Without knowing the details of the agency's affairs she naïvely asked me why I had to work so hard when we had all the money we would ever need. Why, she asked, must you want even more?

I heard the question but didn't sense the depth of her feelings. The idea that she thought what she thought — that we had enough money — and wished what she wished — that I had an ordinary middle-class job keeping ordinary middle-class hours for an ordinary middle-class salary — had never occurred to me. Evidently she hoped — assumed —that after my milestone fortieth birthday I'd spend less time at work and more time at home.

The fateful fortieth.

On the night of that birthday dinner — Thursday the twenty-first of April, nineteen sixty-six — Lily, dressed in an expensive new gown, was apparently making small talk with the babysitter while she waited anxiously for me to get home. But I was stuck. Rose, my secretary, had arranged a surprise after-work party. Not tonight, Rose, I begged as she dragged me up to the roof. Please. But, boss, she said. It's all arranged. Your big four-oh.

Every one of the staff was there, on the roof, waiting to sing 'Happy Birthday' to me. Flares were being lit as autumn darkness was falling over Parnell. There was steak and sausages, beer and boxed wine; and almost everyone was smoking. There was plenty of flirting, too, as most of the staff were young and single, or young and married but wishing they were single. It was, after all, the very middle of the 'swinging sixties'.

Sexy mini-skirted Rose was already a bit 'tiddly' and giggly, and was flattering me shamelessly; flirting more openly than she would dare during the working day. Everyone says I'm *so lucky* to work for *the* Eddie Purvis, she said. But I wasn't interested in Rose; or any other women for that matter. I admired her secretarial skills, and so tolerated her sudden girlishness, but I was annoyed that she hadn't consulted me about the agency party.

Lily had arranged a private room at *The Gourmet* and invited mother, Doris (and Ngaire), and Bill and Penny.

I really wanted to get home in time for that and to see the children before they went to bed. But next thing it was almost seven o'clock. Bill was worried too. He took me aside. I've got to get home and get ready for Lily's dinner, he whispered. Penny'll be wondering where the hell I am. Me too, I said. I gave Lily a ring to say I'd be a bit late. Surely you're not going to be late for your own birthday, she said. Surely not.

She's pretty pissed off, I said to Bill. But look at all this. What the hell can I do? They want me to make a speech, said Bill. Better get it over and done with so we can get away, I said. Anyway, Bill added, they'll be glad when the bosses are gone. At that he moved to the bar, tapped a wine glass with a pen to silence the party, and made a short speech — on behalf of the entire staff of Purvis/Brown Advertising and Marketing, he said — honouring me on my fortieth birthday.

6

A dinner disaster.

I didn't know it then but being late for my absurdly expensive fortieth birthday dinner at *The Gourmet,* that Thursday night in April, nineteen sixty-six, especially arranged by Lily, marked the beginning of an unhappy time in our marriage.

After Bill's speech at the staff party I rang Lily to explain and apologize again. I *couldn't* get away, I said. I mean the trouble they went to. Please understand. But, said an annoyed Lily, your mother and Doris and Ngaire will be there already. I'm supposed to be the hostess. You're the birthday boy. Now I won't be there to greet everyone and you'll be late for your own party. It's a disaster.

Look, I said, I haven't got time to get home and shave and shower and change. I'll go straight there now and be there before you. I'll calm mother down. Don't worry. Jesus, Eddie! said Lily in utter frustration before abruptly hanging up on me.

Bill and I *did* get there before Lily and Penny although mother and Doris (and Ngaire) were already there, waiting. I did manage to explain things to mother who immediately forgave her forty-year-old so successful, so clever, so well dressed, so well groomed, so tall and handsome son. Of course she did.

I smelled of alcohol and smoke, and needed a shave, but she didn't care. She said my thick droopy moustache suited me — I thought so too — and my hair was just the right fashionable length. Thanks to those lovely Beatles, she said. I kissed her on the cheek before rounding the table, cheek-kissing Doris (and Ngaire) in turn before sitting down with Bill while we all waited for Lily and Penny.

When Lily arrived at last, angry and harassed, with a less angry Penny, she slammed a gift-wrapped box on the table in front of me and loud-whispered: Happy birthday, you shit! And, by the way, you stink. Mother did her best to lighten the mood but she wasn't successful. Bill and Penny though made up quickly with a laugh and a light kiss.

What a bloody disaster, I said to Bill the next morning. You can say that again, said Bill. How was Lily later? Pretty shitty, to tell you the truth, I said. How about Penny? Bill shrugged. She was all right, he said. And that was the limit of our birthday dinner discussion. We had plenty else to think about including an invitation to submit for one of the world's biggest cigarette brands; one of the biggest, most high-profile and sought-after accounts in the country.

The affair that wasn't.

As I moved nonchalantly into the first day of my forty-first year, preoccupied with business, Lily was still angry. According to Bill, who later told me what Penny had told him, Lily thought I was having an affair.

He *must* be, she said. She says you're never home. Never take any notice of what the kids are doing. Or what she's up to. Said she feels like an unpaid cleaner and cook. She can't believe you actually *want* to spend so much time at the office so you *must* be having it off with someone.

She thinks it's Rose.

I couldn't believe it. Rose! For Christ's sake, Bill. Don't blame me, said Bill defensively. That's what she thinks. And what did Penny say? I asked. Actually, she laughed, said Bill. Is that it? No, said Bill. She told Lily what I've told her and what I'll tell you again. You work too bloody hard, mate. Never stop. Never stop thinking about work. It's not healthy.

I hadn't heard Bill speak so frankly before. You really think that? I asked. Yep, said Bill. And so does Penny and that's what she told Lily. The only affair you're having is with *business*. She told her. Not just Purvis/Brown but with the whole world of business. The club. Rotary. Chamber of Commerce. The Four As. Every bloody thing. Jesus, I said. I had no idea.

Problems at work and home.

Unfortunately, just when I might have stepped away from business a little, to pay more attention to Lily and the children and all the affairs of home — much as Bill was doing — three things happened to annoy me, occupy even more of my time and attention, and so worsen my problems at home.

Firstly, the agency's serious-minded and exceedingly efficient general manager and director Terry Staines retired in May, just a month after my fortieth birthday; he had joined the agency, as our media manager, in nineteen fifty-three. It took almost the rest of the year to find a suitable replacement. A recruitment agency was tried without success so with Bill's help I set about finding a new general manager; a stressful and time-consuming business. A recently-arrived Englishman, about the same age as Bill and me, with the unlikely name — for an Englishman — of Duane Latrobe, was eventually employed.

Duane's managerial experience was gained at Lintas, in London, which meant that he, like Terry Staines, thoroughly understood the advertising business and its people. He was also, like Terry, utterly sober, affable and honest. As he proved to be perfect in his managerial role he was, a year later, appointed to replace Terry on the small Purvis/Brown board of directors.

Goodbye, Hilda (the tea lady).
Secondly, once Terry had retired the only other employee older than me died suddenly at home one weekend in August. I knew her only as Hilda the tea lady, and although Bill and I, and many others of the staff, went to her funeral I was ashamed to discover how little I knew about one of my oldest employees; oldest in both age and years of service.

You mean she comes to work all the way from out here in Howick? I asked Rose at the funeral. Yes, said Rose. And home. On the bus. Every day.

Hilda's husband was unemployed — actually unemployable as he was somewhat demented and kept wandering away from home — and would have to be cared for by his only daughter. Jesus Christ, we should do something for the daughter, said Bill. We agreed to make a small grant to — What's her name again? I asked. McIlorum, said Bill. Hilda McIlorum — the McIlorum family, or at least what remained of it. Bloody embarrassing though.

As a result of that embarrassment — that is, having to (somewhat reluctantly, I must admit, but apparently sympathetically) fork out for the death of an employee whose name I could barely remember — I got Duane to arrange a blanket insurance policy to cover all staff in the event of death, anywhere, not necessarily at work, which we could use, or choose to not use, in future to cover our embarrassment.

Lily and the car problems.

And, finally, to top off the year, my new car — my dark blue Jaguar S-Type — was rear-ended on a country road in Kaukapakapa by a tractor driven by a stupid farmer who was concentrating more on his cheese and pickle sandwich than watching where he was going.

Never seen a car parked on this road before, he said.

I was parked there while I surveyed my neighbour's for-sale farm. I did buy the farm but sold my small and sporty Jag — it was never the same after that — and bought a very expensive, very large, maroon Jaguar Mark X; all wood and leather and beautiful. But the new car only added to my domestic woes as Lily refused to be seen in it; or let the children ride in it. That other one was bad enough, she said, but this one's ostentatious and ridiculous.

I loved my big Mark X — more, in fact, than I had loved its predecessor — but it caused so much stress, especially as the children couldn't understand why they weren't allowed in 'daddy's lovely new car', that I eventually sold it, for a dreadful loss, to an eye specialist in Kohimarama; I replaced it with a new and neutrally white Ford Fairmont XR.

Well, what do you think? I asked Lily when I parked the Ford it in the drive. It's all right, she said flatly. At least the white matches the house and the roses. I think she still thought I was having an affair.

Television was here but…

By the end of that stressful year — nineteen sixty-six —

Purvis/Brown Advertising and Marketing Limited had not only won one of the country's biggest cigarette accounts but had also become one of the country's biggest television buyers. However, television advertising was then a primitive process which frustrated the hell out of me.

Although filming was done locally — and *everything* was then shot on sixteen-millimetre film using a local company and all local talent — editing and processing had to be done in Australia. That was not only slow but meant that someone — me or my production manager — had to make frequent and expensive return flights to Sydney, often with a client demanding expensive Sydney-side entertainment, to approve each step of the process.

What had once been a novelty — flying to and staying in Sydney — became an expensive and boring chore which no one relished. The result, brought back from Australia, was four small blue cardboard boxes each containing a reel of sixteen millimetre black and white film, one for each station in Auckland, Wellington, Christchurch and Dunedin; networking was not then possible.

Furthermore, all I had learned in Australia, about buying and scheduling television advertising based on audience ratings and research, was wasted in New Zealand. There were no television ratings, and commercials were simply aired randomly at times and in programmes determined by the management of the government-owned and only channel.

The government monopolized radio, too, although Auckland radio listeners, and the advertising industry, joyously celebrated the launch of my friend David Gapes's pirate station, Radio Hauraki, in December, nineteen sixty-six. I wasn't alone in wishing that the government-owned television monopoly could also be broken by a pirate enterprise if only to force efficiencies on what was a dreadful government bureaucracy.

Lily withdraws her support.

My office frustrations faded into the background as Lily's attitude continued to harden despite my determination to spend more time at home. Nothing dramatic happened; Lily seemed to just lose interest in anything but herself and the children.

Whereas she once willingly — happily even — accompanied me to functions and events, whether business or social, she now gently declined to go. You go, Eddie, she would say, pleasantly enough. They — whoever 'they' happened to be — don't want to see me. Yes they do, Lil, I said. And, anyway, I *want* you there. It'll be weird without you. But, said Lily — calmly, reasonably and truthfully — all you ever talk about is: [the agency; the staff; the bank; the client(s); decimal currency; ten o'clock closing; Viet Nam; Holyoake; Norman Kirk; that MacHarmans place; the new committee; the Rotary project; television and radio; etcetera]. It's boring for me, she said. And, anyway: [I've already made tea; it's too late to get a babysitter; John's got a cold; Lisa fell off her bike; I've got nothing to wear; my hair needs doing; I played squash today and I'm stiff; etcetera].

At first I meekly accepted Lily's excuses — I had no choice — and made my own excuses for her absence. Eventually, though, her non-attendance at business-related functions came to be taken for granted by everyone. It must have been obvious that something was wrong at home although no one cared to ask what that 'something' might be.

Lisa starts school. Lily wants a job.

Lisa joined John at Takapuna Primary after the nineteen sixty-seven August school holidays. Then, suddenly, Lily had no role at Playcentre which had been part of her social life for two years. It was a vacuum she found hard to fill. She said she was thinking of getting a little job. Like Penny, she said. What the hell for? I asked. Meet people and that, she said. Get out of the house. The kids are at school almost all day. It'll be interesting.

I didn't like the idea, and said so, so she did nothing about it. She and Penny Brown remained friends although they saw less of each as Penny *was* working part time somewhere. A coffee shop in High Street I think.

The next few years hurried by but little changed for Lily and me; we just continued to do our own separate things. The agency's growth slowed somewhat, at least in terms of its client list and staff numbers, but organic growth, without more overheads or expenses, meant more profit. Gradually I found I had less to do with day-to-day management as Duane Latrobe and Bill Brown's shared stewardship, with Tom Wolfendale's continued oversight, ensured that Purvis/Brown became and remained one of the country's most successful advertising agencies.

The winds of change.

With more time on my hands I was able to be more active in the wider business and advertising communities. Then, as a more active member of what was then known as the 4As — the Association of Accredited Advertising Agencies — I saw two worrying trends.

First was the emergence of a new generation of advertising entrepreneurs; young men unscarred by childhood poverty and memories of depression and war.

They were part of what became known as 'the swinging sixties', a period that saw a creative revolution in all things cultural including — above all as far as I was concerned — advertising. In America — the spiritual and *actual* home of modern advertising — Doyle Dane Bernbach and Ogilvy & Mather, in particular but amongst others, were amazing their more conservative competitors with their creativity and success.

I saw the equivalent rise of breath-taking creativity in New Zealand. For example, *Damn the Dam,* a hit song of protest, written and sung by a young John Hanlon whom I knew vaguely, began life as part of an energy-conservation advertising campaign for an insulating batts brand, while the political propaganda advertising for the resurgent Labour Party emerged from a hitherto obscure but ultimately audacious young Bob Harvey and his small but aggressive advertising agency, MacHarman Associates. Harvey's nineteen sixty-nine Norman Kirk Labour Party campaign, while ultimately unsuccessful, shook both the New Zealand political and advertising scenes and was followed by an unqualified success at the nineteen seventy-two election.

The second unmissable and somewhat related trend was the entry into New Zealand of the world's largest and most influential (and always American) advertising agency brands. Although New Zealand law didn't allow outright foreign ownership it didn't stop a local agency linking up — sometimes in name only — with an American agency. The intentional result was that the American agency at home could offer a New Zealand service to their increasingly international-minded clients while the New Zealand agency would not only gain a profitable new American account but would also gain access to the parent agency's vast resources and professional advice as well as, incidentally, bathing in the reflected glory of having or adding the name of its American partner.

I recognized these related trends and knew that Duane, Bill and I couldn't suddenly reinvent ourselves. I knew that, compared with the young men leading Auckland's version of advertising's creative revolution, we, approaching fifty years old, were considered part of the conservative establishment.

Suddenly Purvis/Brown's remarkable growth stalled. Suddenly it became harder to attract new business and young creative staff. Suddenly it was impossible to win new advertising accounts which were tied to an American master agency. Suddenly we were in danger of losing our big cigarette account.

I knew, suddenly, that something had to be done. But what?

Introducing America's oldest advertising agency.

One morning, at the end of nineteen seventy-two, an elderly — at least I considered him elderly at the time — American man, friendly, distinguished, white-haired, tall with an almost military bearing, walked into the agency, without an appointment, and asked to see the managing director. He introduced himself as Cam Worth although, according to his card, he was Cameron Montgomery Worth, Jnr., Director (Retired), N. W. Ayer Advertising, Inc., Avenue of the Americas, New York, N.Y.

Over coffee in the boardroom he told me he had been brought out of retirement to scope Pacific-rim countries for local advertising agencies to represent N. W. Ayer. His agency was expected to win a big international account — I'd rather not disclose the identity of the party at this time, he said — which required a seamless international advertising service. Our potential client has a presence on every continent, in almost every country in the world, he said. So we — he meant his agency — need to show we have a mirroring international network acting for us from New York.

I'll go ahead and be completely honest, he said later. Yours is not the only Auckland agency I'm interviewing. I nodded, understanding that anything could happen but hoping that Purvis/Brown Advertising and Marketing Limited might soon be a branch office of N. W. Ayer, America's oldest advertising agency which, for some reason, had not bothered about the rest of the world until now. The meeting ended with me escorting Cam Worth down to the street where we shook hands on the understanding — nothing was in writing — that he would be in touch, one way or the other.

Apart from actually liking Cam Worth, a liking that was evidently mutual, I had to be neutral about the potential for an international relationship with his agency. I hardly dared imagine all the benefits; the most immediate would be the painless acquisition of a large American client. I remembered what Cam had said: Our potential client has a presence on every continent, in almost every country in the world.

Shit, Eddie, said Bill Brown without hesitation, it's Pan Am. No question. It's all over *Advertising Age*. I saw that, I said, remembering. According to them, said Bill, Ayer are expected to piss in.

A big American partner and a big new account.

One morning three months later I got a phone call from Cam Worth, followed by a confirming telex, telling me that N. W. Ayer had been officially appointed advertising agency for the world by Pan American World Airways, and that the Ayer board of directors had accepted his recommendation that Purvis/Brown

Advertising and Marketing Limited be appointed Ayer's New Zealand partner. Jerry Bock, Ayer's executive vice-president for the Pacific, would be flying out within days to get things started.

Suddenly there was a lot to do. There was an agency announcement and rooftop party. There were interviews with *National Business Review, The New Zealand Herald* as well as *Marketing, Ad-Media* and *Management* magazines.

Later there was a directors' dinner at the *Top of The Town*. Lily *did* attend on that occasion which was only part celebration; I thought it important that everyone, including the directors' wives, should be aware of what the Ayer association would mean for the agency's long-term future. But whatever they all thought, whatever else happened, I hoped above all that I'd get Lily's support. I hoped she was proud of my achievements but I wasn't really sure what she thought or felt. As for the others: I didn't know what they thought. But nor did I really care.

For myself I saw the opportunity to reduce my day-to-day management of Purvis/Brown and increase my involvement with the N. W. Ayer network, perhaps becoming part of the international management team. International travel — with Lily, I hoped — appealed. I also knew that the American giant would eventually want to buy part — perhaps all — of the agency which would then turn my years of work into a massive cash windfall, enough to set up Lily and me for the rest of our lives.

In the short term, though, I was looking forward to meeting Ayer's executive vice-president (Account Supervisor, Pacific, for the Pan Am account), Jerry Bock, who was expected at the agency within days.

Business was booming.

By the end of that year Purvis/Brown's relationship with both N. W. Ayer in New York and the local Pan Am management team was working well. The sudden and huge addition of Pan Am's work and billings added almost nothing to overheads, except for the employment of Duane's choice of account executive for Pan Am and the expense of moving him and his family from Paris.

In fact business was booming. The Pan Am acquisition had attracted more international accounts, the agency's reputation had never been better, all eighty-five employees were happy and proud of the agency and its high profile. Bill and I each had a new car, a Ford Fairlane, our third Ford since moving our business to John W. Andrew. Lily, too, had a new car, a sporty little Mini Clubman, which she loved to drive; she *really* enjoyed driving.

Lily starts to understand.

Most importantly, the agency's relationship with Ayer and Pan Am happily brought about a change in Lily's attitude to me, the agency and the whole advertising business. It felt as though she properly understood why I enjoyed my work so much when in June we were invited to New York to meet the Ayer board as well as the principals of Ayer's other international partners.

A tour of the agency's office, towering high over the Avenue of the America's, with breath-taking views of upper Manhattan and Central Park was followed by a Friday night dinner, in that very park, at the famous *Tavern on the Green*.

At the preceding cocktail party, the long and exceedingly lavish dinner which followed, and the Sunday visit to the president's Hampton Bays summer house, she came to meet, know and like — a feeling that was mutual — many of the international principals' wives including that of the company president himself, the vice-president for the Pacific, and the exceedingly wealthy, posh-sounding but thoroughly down-to-earth wife of someone important and titled from Ayer's London partner, Charles Barker, where, I remembered, Irma-Leigh Colherne had once worked.

We stayed — Lily insisted we should — at the Algonquin Hotel. Oh, Penny, she said later, to her friend, it was absolutely wonderful. Dorothy Parker and all that. And when I was busy at meetings she and the other wives toured New York's famous galleries.

One night — a highlight — we went to see *Death of a Salesman* at the Vivian Beaumont. Lily was suddenly in her element.

A man (and woman) of the world.

Over the next couple of years I often travelled to and from New York, negotiating the sale of a minority interest in the agency, helped by Tom Wolfendale and my lawyer, Reece William, QC. In the process I came to acquire a taste for first-class air travel, and everything it delivered beyond a comfortable seat, including the finest in French food and wines served in a first-class Pan Am cabin as well as at the finest restaurants in New York. Sometimes it was necessary to meet in Los Angeles, San Francisco, Toronto, London, Frankfurt, Vienna, Paris or Rome, depending on the schedule of Ayer's negotiators in those cities.

On those occasions I made sure Lily came with me to see what I saw, and learn what I learned, at the world's finest hotels and restaurants. With plenty of free time, while I was busy, she soon became a well-travelled and experienced woman of the world.

An agreement to sell part of the agency to Ayer was eventually reached at the beginning of nineteen seventy-six. At the end of April that year, Tom Wolfendale, Reece Williams and I set off for New York where I signed the deal that would give Ayer a twenty-five per cent share of the agency, turn it into Purvis/Brown/Ayer Advertising International, and in the process deliver more money into my bank account than I had ever dreamed possible.

And then, suddenly, in New York, just as I was going to celebratory lunch with the others, I got a phone call from Lily.

7

'*...your wife is on the phone.*'

I was standing alone, at the wall-to-wall floor-to-ceiling windows of Ayer's cool and silent forty-fourth floor boardroom, gazing at the view up the bright-green-with-Spring length of Central Park. It was an amazing sight: Central Park West to one side, Fifth Avenue to the other, the whole of upper Manhattan laid out like a silent model city. While it really was — still is I suppose — an astonishing view, I was more astonished to realize that it was now a familiar cityscape.

I was waiting for Tom Wolfendale and Reece Williams. I remember, it was Wednesday the twenty-eighth of April, a few days after my fiftieth birthday which I had experienced twice: once in Auckland and then again in Los Angeles. We were to have lunch at the painfully posh and expensive *Sign of The Dove*, with Cam, Nico — who was responsible for the negotiations — and Jerry, as guests of Lou Martinelli, Ayer's president.

I heard the door open at the distant end of the room and turned, expecting to see Jerry, Tom and Reece. Instead, a middle-aged woman — smartly dressed and efficient looking — came in and walked briskly down the length of the thickly-carpeted room. She obviously had something for me: a message? I walked towards her and we met in the middle, beside the long board table.

Mr Purvis, she said quietly. It seems your wife is on the phone.

That was a shock. Now? I asked. I looked at my new watch — a double rolled gold Cartier I had bought in Fifth Avenue only the day before, a birthday treat — quickly calculating the time in New Zealand: just after five o'clock Thursday morning. She's on the phone now? I asked again. Oh, yes, said the lady secretary. Waiting on the phone. Go ahead and take it in my office. I have another errand. It'll be quiet there. This way please, Mr Purvis.

She must have sensed something perturbing about the phone call because once she had shown me to her office — a wood-panelled ante-room of the boardroom — she didn't return, at least not for as long as I sat in her chair. Her name, according to the wooden desk-wedge nameplate, was Dolores Gray. But although I had picked it up, turned it over and over in my hand, stroked its green baize base, my confused mind did not register that it carried the name of the woman in whose chair I was sitting, at her desk, in her office, where I had just hung up the phone after talking to Lily. I had almost forgotten where I was — in New York — and why.

Shocking news from far away.

Oh, Eddie, said Lily from far away. I'm sorry. I couldn't sleep. It's awful. I don't know… Her voice was shaking; she sounded awful. What is it, Lil? I asked nervously. Tell me. What's happening? Oh, Eddie, I'm so sorry but… But what? It's so hard, she said. It's, well, your mother died last night, Eddie. She had a heart attack. I don't know exactly when. She rang up Doris. Crying. Doris and Ngaire went…

And so it went on. Lily talking in a rush. The

ambulance. The hospital. The doctors. The police. The horror and hopelessness of it all. Me listening but not quite believing. And then, suddenly, I heard Lily say: But, Eddie, listen, what will you do? I'll come home, I said quietly. Now. Right now. And then I sat, slumped in Dolores Gray's chair, in her quiet office on the fortieth-fourth floor of N. W. Ayer's building on the Avenue of the Americas, New York, turning over her name-plate in my hands, numb, thinking nothing, until the office door opened quietly, slowly and slightly, and Tom Wolfendale's puzzled and worried face appeared in the gap.

Rushing home.

Ayer's travel office and Pan Am together ensured there was no delay in my getting home. A bit more than twenty-fours hours after Lily's call I was sitting in her Mini, on a chilly autumn morning, speeding up the harbour bridge. I felt exhausted. I remembered nothing of the desperate trip across the continent to Los Angeles and then the twelve-hour flight across the black Pacific, non-stop thanks to Pan Am's 'SP' service. I slept poorly, despite the first-class comfort, and ate almost nothing of the superb dinner service; and then not even breakfast.

Speaking of foolish things, inconsequential and inappropriate, as grieving and stressed people do, I said to the grimly concentrating Lily: You know how much I — we — used to love first class. Well, it was a complete waste this trip. Just as well I didn't have to pay for it.

And then, as we passed through the bridge toll gates, I suddenly thought to ask: How are the kids? They're home, waiting for us. Grace's with them. I was surprised. Really? Grace? Yes, said Lily. Grace. No school today? I asked. What do *you* think, Eddie? Lily asked indignantly. They're sad, Eddie. Can't you see that? Their grandmother. Their only grandparent. I nodded slowly, glumly, unwilling to remind Lily that Grace was also their grandmother.

Doris (and Ngaire) were also waiting for us so I learned exactly what happened after mother's crying-with-fear-and-pain middle-of-the-night phone call and their rushed trip to McCullouch Avenue.

Mother's funeral.

Nearly thirty-five years a widow, said the minister. That surprised the hell out of me. A widow. I hadn't thought of my father for years.

Anyway, during my absence and blankness Doris (and Ngaire) had made all the arrangements for mother's funeral and burial. Evidently when Catherine-Ann died, and later my father, we were so poor that mother had to accept the Waikumete burial plots assigned by the city. But — as I discovered only much later — when mother died Ngaire had some important job at the city council and had arranged for Catherine-Ann and Quentin's coffins, or what remained of them and their contents, to be reburied with mother in a new location chosen by the church. It must have cost a fortune but apparently Doris paid. It was only then I learned that Doris was no longer the manager of that narrow little McKenzies store in Karangahape Road; she was that company's Northern Regional Manager.

Lutheran, I said, in surprise, when I learned details of the funeral. I never knew she went to church. Just shows you, said Doris sarcastically. What do you mean? I asked indignantly. It's typical of you, Eddie, she said angrily; I noticed that Lily nodded (almost imperceptibly) in silent agreement. Do you ever think of poor Catherine-Ann? How mama felt when her little girl died? And papa?

What about him? You just thought he was a drunk didn't you. Well he was a good man, a good father, a good husband, before all that. Have you any idea what he went through for us? And mama? The struggles? As for mama, you thought because you had money, gave her money and things, that's all she needed. That you were being a good son. Think again, Eddie Purvis. Doris sounded really bitter. Your mother, she continued. Your wife. Your lovely children. Grace. Even me and Ngaire. What do you *really* know about any of us? Really?

My big 'announcement'.

A week later Lily arranged a family dinner in a well-meaning attempt to bring us together after mother's funeral. Although we all tried hard to be jolly, especially for the sake of John and Lisa, things were never quite the same between me and my older sister who shared many of my Freeman's Bay memories. Strangely, though, the atmosphere of lingering sadness about our mother was not unpleasant; was even cherished.

The dinner was also a platform for my big 'announcement' which surprised everyone but Lily. Actually, it was *not* an announcement but a quiet talk from a seated me at the head of the table. You're not the big boss at the agency now, Lily had insisted, taking her plain-speaking lead from Doris, so keep it informal, Eddie, eh. Just a chat. Shall I stand up? I asked. No! insisted Lily. Absolutely not! There's only the seven of us for God's sake.

Once sixteen-year-old John (a sixth former at Takapuna Grammar), and Lisa (almost fourteen, also a Takapuna Grammarian), heard they were going on a family trip to America they heard — or at least understood — nothing else. I told them we would be going to Disneyland and Universal Studios and Knott's

Berry Farm and all the places they'd heard about from their friends; and then to New York and Washington where none of their friends had been. That was it as far as they were concerned.

But *that* trip, to be taken with the children in the coming May holidays, was only Part One of my important talk to the family. Losing mama like that, I said, so suddenly, when I wasn't even home, was a real shock. I know she was seventy-one but I thought she was pretty well. I was speaking mainly to Doris then but was finding it therapeutic to talk to *anyone; to simply talk.* I went on: Turns out she wasn't well at all but I didn't know that. But *you* did, Dossy, you knew that and so much more and I didn't and I'm sorry.

I went on, telling the table — Doris (and Ngaire), Grace and the non-listening children — what I'd already told Lily. Now that the deal with Ayer is done I'm taking the rest of the year off. It's all arranged. When we've finished the trip to the States next month, with you two — I was speaking to John and Lisa then — mum and I are going to carry on and do a world trip. Six whole months off, eh. How about that?

What I didn't say about the future, when our trip was over — because Lily and I were still debating it — was that New York had offered me Jerry Bock's position as Ayer's vice-president for Asia based in Singapore. Jerry's moving to Frankfurt, I told Lily, so it's a fantastic opportunity. But Lily protested: There's no way we're moving to Singapore, she said. The kids have got school. Then university. I don't like the idea at all, Eddie.

We agreed to say nothing to the children, to make no quick decision, but to think about it — discuss it — while we were away. At least that's what I thought we had agreed but I was beginning to see that in the end Lily would never move to Singapore.

Would I have to go alone?

The family in America.

For a fourteen-year-old New Zealand girl and her sixteen-year-old brother to travel first class to, from and around America in nineteen seventy-six, staying in the finest hotels, was an experience then beyond the imagination of even most New Zealand adults. And although they thought they were a bit old for Disneyland they managed to enjoy themselves there and even more at the other attractions, sites, towns, cities, hotels and restaurants they visited — often travelling in a big American car — during their two-week jaunt.

They were especially feted on their visit to Ayer's New York headquarters where they charmed everyone with their quaint courtesy and 'darling' accents. And they were left breathless by the view from the company's forty-fourth floor boardroom — I showed Lily Dolores Gray's office where I had taken her phone call about mother — and then even more breathless, if that were possible, by the view from the *Windows on the World* restaurant at the top of the North Tower of the new but doomed World Trade Center.

At the end of the tour Lily and I left John and Lisa in the care of an Ayer nurse who escorted them to Los Angeles for their flight back to Auckland where they were met by Penny Brown. They stayed with the Browns in Narrow Neck until we returned just before Christmas. It was a happy arrangement for them as they'd always been friends with Tui and Riki Brown who also went to Takapuna Grammar.

Lily in her element in Europe.

Lily and I travelled around Europe mostly by train, occasionally by coach or hire car, staying as long as we (actually, Lily) liked in each city, depending how much time we (she) needed to see what we (she) most wanted to see, stopping in only the best hotels which we (Lily) had chosen in advance. No major European city was missed — including those of Scandinavia and Russia — as Lily tried to tick off every possible art gallery, museum, cathedral, castle, Roman ruin, palace, stately home, theatre and opera house along the way.

How do you know about all these places? I asked early in our progress. All this arty stuff? Because, Eddie, she replied, while you've been at the office all the hours God sends I've been reading and watching television and videos, and going to galleries and concerts and talking to people in the know and finding out about all this 'arty stuff' as you call it.

In the beginning I was restless but tried not to show it. But as we settled into a routine I began to relax, to forget about what might or might not be happening at the agency. I enjoyed, especially, the quiet dinners with Lily each evening, at a place and setting which were invariably beautiful, romantic, and expensive. Then I enjoyed settling down in our hotel room with our *Frommer's* to plan the next day in detail and week in general.

Wherever we were I noticed that Lily — tall, blonde and beautiful as ever at forty-six — always caught the eye of others, especially men. She always looked elegant, poised, confident and at ease, as though she 'belonged' in Europe and had always known the best places to be and be seen. She, though, seemed innocently unaware of her effect on others. She seemed to be happy just to be away with me, to sense our marriage being repaired, and to see how I admired her and her knowledge.

That knowledge *did* impress me and underlined my own *lack* of knowledge and appreciation. I realized then that although it was my natural aptitude for drawing and accurate draughtsmanship which had led me into the *business* of commercial art, I did not, in the end, care for fine art, artists and art history, just as I didn't really care, as Lily did, for the great architects, composers, writers, dramatists, politicians and warriors who had made the great civilization of Europe which I, as a citizen of the world, had inherited and should have appreciated.

As I became aware of all that — introspection possible only because of the enforced absence from work — I was not immediately aware of Lily's admiration for *me*. I learned of it only gradually, as we talked over long dinners in some of Europe's most romantic places. I learned, for example, that she still admired me for *my* distinguished looks; my height and manly bearing; my greying hair; my grooming and tasteful wardrobe; and how I, too, in her opinion, looked every bit a man of the sophisticated nineteen-seventies world, at ease in any company, anywhere.

But more than that, she said, she admired me — and, yes, loved me — for my determination to succeed in business, despite the poverty and disadvantages of my Freeman's Bay childhood, and for the way I had never denied her and the children anything except, perhaps, my time and attention for which she now forgave me. Our once-in-a-lifetime journey turned out to be a journey of discovery in more ways than one.

In the process of that journey I also discovered the homesickness I'd never felt before and had scorned in others. I was actually looking forward to getting home and spending more time there with my beautiful and clever wife and my children who were on the brink of adulthood and whose childhood I had almost missed.

One night at dinner — we were dining outside, lakeside, at our *Lago Como* hotel — I reached across the table, covered Lily's long and narrow hand with mine, and said simply: I'm not going to take the Singapore job, love. It was the first and only time either of us had raised the matter. Lily looked up from stirring her *Negroni*, smiled gently, and said: That's good, Eddie. I'm glad. And that was that.

Meanwhile, at home.

While we were away things had happened to the Brown family which not only changed their lives but would also affect me, my business, my financial affairs, my family, and my Bill Brown friendship.

It began — as I learned later from John and Lisa, who were staying with the Browns at the time — when Penny's Auntie Hine died. While Penny's mother Marama had married a Pākehā, living and raising her family in Point Chevalier, her Auntie Hine had married Henare Te Kawau Tawera Kennedy who became a respected kaumātua at Ōrākei.

What I learned only later — variously from Lily and Lisa and Bill himself — was that during Auntie Hine's illness and hospitalization, after her death, at the tangi and later, Bill had become aware of a stirring resentment on the Ōrākei marae which was somehow related to his own Dargaville marae. After hearing what he called 'the sad history' of the Ōrākei people, evidently described so eloquently by Penny's Uncle Henare and, especially, by his friend Joe Hawke, Bill and Penny decided to do whatever they could to support the protest which Joe Hawke was planning for the new year.

As nineteen seventy-six turned to nineteen seventy-seven, and I began to think again of the Purvis/Brown/Ayer Advertising business in New Zealand, Bill Brown was deciding — with Penny's support — to *reduce* his presence and activity at the agency. He said it was his turn to take some time off and he was going to join the protest at Bastion Point. He was going to camp there for as long as necessary. I couldn't figure that out. Why do you want to hang out with those bloody communists? I asked. Bill just shook his head slowly, hopelessly I thought, and said: They're not communists, Eddie.

I wasn't especially worried by Bill's decision and pending absence. Like most people, I didn't think much about Māori grievances; I thought the Bastion Point occupation would be a short-lived thing and that Bill would soon be back at work.

I was heartened and, I must admit, mildly humiliated, when I learned, at the company's first board meeting of the new year, that the agency was now so big, successful and well managed that I was hardly missed during my absence. Evidently there were some new staff — amongst a crew then numbering almost a hundred — who had never met me. It feels a bit weird, I said to Lily. Some of the young ones don't even know who I am. Lily was delighted. It means you're becoming dispensable, she said. You'll be able to get out when you're ready and the agency will just carry on without you. Who said anything about getting out? I asked. One day, said Lily with a smile. One day. When you're ready.

I thought then that if I hadn't been missed for six months then Bill Brown would hardly be missed for a few weeks. In fact, though, Bill, who had quietly reverted to his real name — Wiremu Paraone — was away for the entire nineteen seventy-seven year and much of the next. But I was right: the agency was big enough to manage without him. Or me.

I spent the next few years travelling around Asia and the Pacific on Ayer/Pan Am business. Lily was disappointed; I had, after all, declined the Singapore job and promised to spend more time at home. But what can I do? I protested. They haven't appointed anyone to Singapore so they're relying on me. You're being used, Eddie, said Lily cynically.

When she could, when I was home, Lily tried to tell me about Bastion Point, and how it was affecting Bill and Penny and their children. But I wasn't interested. Well, said Lily, if you don't care, if you don't take notice of what's going on, you'll lose Bill as a business partner *and* a friend. My response was always the same: It'll all be over soon, love, I said.

I changed my mind when Bill was one of two hundred or so protesters evicted and arrested on that dramatic day in May, nineteen seventy-eight.

While I was away.

They've gone already? I asked, surprised and hurt that my old friend hadn't waited to say goodbye. You've been gone nearly six weeks, said Lily. All the same, I said defensively. Bill's got ties in Dargaville, said Lily, so they've shifted up there. Tui and Riki too. Leaving all this Auckland bullshit behind. What bullshit? I asked. I don't know, said Lily. That's what Penny said. Said they want to get back to their Māori roots. Penny's not Māori, I protested. Of course she is, said a surprised Lily. They're both Ngāti Whātua. *And* the kids. Can't you tell? Are you blind or something, Eddie? I never noticed, I said, which was true. Never even thought about it.

I thought about it then, though. I thought about Willy, the little Māori kid I used to play with in Freeman's Bay. And then, later, when Willy became Bill and we got together again. When was that? About nineteen fifty-six, I thought. Bill joining the agency, then the board, being such a great asset, supervising new business. I remembered how we met Lily and Penny at the same dance. Then our double wedding — on the twenty-fifth of January, nineteen fifty-eight, a date I could not, dare not, forget — and having kids, a boy and a girl each, about the same time. And then, out of nowhere, all this Māori stuff. Where the hell did that come from?

Nevertheless, once Bill left the agency, once he and the family had left Auckland for Dargaville, I didn't do anything to contact him. A bit slack I suppose. One good thing though: Tui and Lisa always kept up their friendship.

8

Redundant at work. Redundant at home.

My tripping around Asia stopped when New York appointed someone from the San Francisco office to the Singapore job. Suddenly I was almost redundant. The office, under Duane Latrobe's management, had learned to function without me and Bill. In fact when attending meetings I often felt out of my depth so I just kept my mouth shut. I was pleased to learn that my silence was taken as understanding and approval, and that clients seemed to be impressed by the mere presence of Eddie Purvis at 'their' meeting.

This virtual redundancy meant that for the first time in years I had time on my hands; time to spend at home with Lily and the (no longer) children except the (no longer) children were no longer at home: John was at Otago university and Lisa was spending a year with a friend in Melbourne before starting at Auckland university in nineteen eighty.

I was almost redundant at home too. During the years of my absence — at first obsessed with growing the agency and later with so much international travel — Lily had run the household. She was used to managing all the regular monthly accounts as well as large annual bills, and arranging house and garden maintenance. All this as well as routine housekeeping including shopping, cooking, feeding and clothes-shopping for two growing children — and for me sometimes — while keeping up an active social life.

I can't even do the lawns, I said one fine February Saturday in that first year of virtual redundancy. There's no mower. I sold it years ago, said Lily. I use Ernie and Beth and they've got their own ride-on mower. Who's Ernie and Beth? was my obvious question. They look after the lawns and garden and hedges and stuff, said Lily. Do the windows and gutters. Even wash the house when it's needed. Since when? I asked. Since they started their business, gardening and lawns and that, replied Lily. Nineteen sixty-six. When John started school and you seemed to lose interest in anything but work.

As it happened I was lucky to be redundant at work because suddenly, at the beginning of nineteen eighty-one, I was desperately needed at home. Indeed, for the next few years my presence at home was so important I spent almost no time at the office; before long I was permanently absent.

The cause of this dramatic change of circumstances was not pleasant — not easy to talk about — but it must be recorded.

Lily's inheritance from her unknown father.

My darling Lily (Lillian Dawn Purvis, nee Braithwaite) died in August nineteen eighty-five; she was just fifty-five years old. Her death came after more than four years of a debilitating illness which appeared to come on suddenly but was in fact inherited.

I learned only later that Lily had been secretly worried about her mysterious symptoms before telling me. Her condition became progressively worse, quickly, until she was confined to a wheelchair, unable to do almost anything for herself. Eventually she was bedridden, requiring constant professional nursing. At last, early in the morning of Sunday the twenty-sixth of August, nineteen eighty-five, she died peacefully in Auckland hospital. I was there with a broken-hearted Lisa and a brave John who had flown in from his new home in America.

Lily's death was the source of more family anguish and grief than might be thought normal because we learned that not only was her illness inherited from a parent but also that it might have been bequeathed to her children.

When her symptoms appeared, and then seemed to get worse quickly, Lily was referred to a specialist who immediately diagnosed her problem and gave his gloomy prognosis. There was no cure, and treatment was limited to pain relief with devices and braces to support weakened muscles in the neck and limbs. A wheelchair was inevitable as was confinement to bed, hospital and, eventually, sooner rather than later, death.

At first Lily was angry; angry with the world; angry with Grace (for one obvious reason); angry with me for leaving her to run *everything* for years; just plain angry.

Her anger didn't last; she was naturally cheerful and optimistic. It quickly mutated into a profound and tearful sadness, clinging tightly, desperately, to me, wanting me always to be near, and seeing everyone and everything familiar — at home and around Takapuna — through a misty veil of melancholia, as if for the last time. I heard her, often, saying her goodbyes aloud. Goodbye, kitchen. Goodbye, Gretchen and Dick (to her beloved Gretchen Albrecht and Dick Frizzell paintings). Goodbye, books. Goodbye, garden. Goodbye, Hall's Corner. Goodbye, Minehaha and your beautiful old pōhutukawas. Goodbye, beach. Goodbye, badminton club and squash courts. Goodbye, John, my darling clever boy. Goodbye Lisa, my precious. Please God you will both escape this horrible thing. Goodbye, Eddie. Despite everything, I still love you with all my heart. How on earth will you cope without me? Goodbye, world.

Before long, though, there were no tears, no sadness, no goodbyes, nothing but hours, days, weeks and months of pain and medication, and a complete loss of independence and dignity. Everyone agreed: when the end came it was a huge relief.

The end of Grace.

Immediately she was told about the source of Lily's illness, Grace — by then an old and unhappy seventy-year-old living alone in the Braithwaite family home in Point Chevalier — sank into a deep depression; she contemplated suicide. As neither she, her father or mother had carried Lily's disease, she and everyone realized that Lily must have inherited it from her unknown father, Grace's unremembered once-only lover.

Whoever he was he'll be dead by now, said Lily's consultant when he learned that the identity of Lily's father was not (and would never be) known.

Grace not only — and, I thought, correctly — blamed her promiscuous fourteen-year-old self for innocent Lily's horrible illness and death but she also knew, with unbearable guilt, that one or both of Lily's children — who still thought of her as their aunt rather than their grandmother — might be doomed to the same illness and early death.

Grace didn't take her own life then — which, anyway, was virtually taken from her as a child by her unknown lover and unforgiving parents — but soon after Lily's death was found to be incurably depressed, on the verge of insanity, and was confined to a private clinic in Epsom. I paid for her treatment there; she was not missed, received no visitors, and died, on the second anniversary of Lily's death, from an overdose of prescribed sleeping pills which she had secretly collected.

What about John and Lisa?

When Lily's illness was diagnosed — at the beginning of nineteen eighty-one — John and Lisa were taken by surprise. Lily had managed to hide her symptoms from them which wasn't hard as John was away at Otago university and Lisa, while living at home after her year in Australia, was studying at Auckland university and, anyway, was otherwise preoccupied with boys — especially one — and having fun. She rarely saw Lily, spent little time in her company, and so, in the beginning, didn't notice anything wrong. Lily and I waited until Easter that year, when John and Lisa were home for the holidays, to tell them.

The hardest part to tell, and for them to hear, was the possibility that one or both of them might have inherited Lily's awful disease. But where did mum get it from? was their obvious question. Lily then had to explain the strange circumstances of her birth: that her apparent sister was actually her mother; that her apparent mother was actually her grandmother; that their Aunt Grace was actually their grandmother and that their late grandmother would have been their *great*-grandmother.

Grace made a terrible mistake, said a sick, sad but unbelievably sympathetic Lily adding, prophetically: It's something she's now finding impossible to live with. At a later family conference at the hospital, with Lily's consultant, John and Lisa learned that — based on only the flimsiest of available research — their chances of inheriting their mother's disease were thought to be about fifty-fifty.

John.

By the time Lily died John was working as an assistant track and field coach at some university in America. He came home for the funeral but stayed in a hotel and spent as little time as possible with me, Lisa, Grace, Doris (and Ngaire). I assumed he had loved his mother all his life — as a son usually loves his mother, as I had loved mine — but he seemed to find it impossible to share his grief, especially with me. In fact he seemed to have not even a grudging respect for me, and hardly acknowledged the care I had happily provided Lily during her last helpless years.

He did report however — to me and Lisa, and his Aunt Doris (and Ngaire), and to a hugely relieved Grace — that tests carried out for him in America had found no sign of Lily's *myotonic dystrophy*; he said he was fit and healthy, felt well, and definitely had no symptoms. A week later he flew back to America and was never again seen in New Zealand.

Lisa.

Lisa confirmed that she too had been found free of the disease. So far anyway, she said to the family.

She was living in Ponsonby then, with her fiancé. She had qualified and was working as a junior accountant for Tom Wolfendale's firm, Wolfendale Mills, which still shared the same Parnell building with Purvis/Brown/Ayer Advertising.

When Lily died Lisa was both devastated and relieved. She had loved and admired Lily but, unlike John, had no difficulty sharing her grief. Like John, she had also grown distant from me, but unlike John was then grateful for the way I had nursed Lily. When John went back to America she was left alone to worry and care for me as best she could. However, it was a burden too heavy.

It had been an exhausting few years for Lisa and it was only later, when I was finally left alone in the big Minehaha house, that she allowed herself to collapse. Her grief was extreme; medication was prescribed and she was off work for two months. So severe was her breakdown that her fiancé — an electrician called Colin Watt, (yes, Watt), who was in the process (with Lisa's financial advice and help) of starting his own little business — threatened to leave. He didn't leave but their wedding was postponed indefinitely.

Doris.

Throughout the whole of Lily's ordeal Doris might have been able to support me more but she didn't. Like John and Lisa, her nephew and niece, she had, over the years, and for some reason, grown distant from me despite our shared childhood and family history. As far as I can remember there had been no sudden break in our once-close relationship. Rather, once mother died it seemed we had nothing in common.

Doris enjoyed her work where she was evidently esteemed by the Wellington management who rewarded her with employment security, an excellent salary, certain fringe benefits, and a generous annual bonus. All the same, she once said her income was probably a pittance compared to what she imagined I earned and was worth. But unlike me she was content with her work, her income and her personal life. Thanks to Ngaire's political contacts, influence and ungentle nature, the two of them were together able to raise and afford a mortgage on a Herne Bay flat, an almost unheard-of achievement for women at that time.

In many ways plain Doris was the opposite of the blonde, beautiful, warm and amiable Lily. But in fact they had been as close as sisters, each admiring in the other what she herself lacked. Lily's illness therefore brought Doris even closer to her sister-in-law meaning she saw me then at my home-based and caring best. But when, finally, Lily was there no more Doris turned to the strong arms of Ngaire for comfort and support. I rarely saw Doris (and Ngaire) after that.

Learning new skills.

In the beginning, for the first few months of her illness, Lily insisted on maintaining her independence. Because she remained remarkably cheerful then I felt obliged to hide my own worries and pretend to be as optimistic as she appeared to be. Before long, though, she became less able, in more pain, so that although I employed a professional nurse — who stayed nights when Lily was especially poorly — I chose to spend more time at home. Eventually I found more reasons to stay home all day, fewer reasons to go to the office, which meant I lost touch with the business altogether. I soon realized I was becoming a liability — especially in face-to-face meetings with clients and staff — so I limited my involvement to attending board meetings; even there I surrendered the chair to Tom Wolfendale.

Meanwhile I learned an entirely new suite of home management skills. I could have employed a team of professionals but poor sick Lily didn't want to be surrounded by strangers, doing all the work while she could do nothing, so I decided to learn everything necessary to make her life as comfortable as possible.

My teachers were Lily herself — who, in the beginning, instructed me, even from her bed — Lisa, Doris (and Ngaire), and the nurse. The subjects in which I received coaching included everything to do with running a house — shopping, cooking, washing, ironing and housework in general — as well as supervising Lily's gardeners and employing miscellaneous tradesmen, when necessary, choosing them from Lily's phone index. I also had to pay the household bills, a monthly chore I detested.

Although I didn't know it then, they were all lessons which, as a widower, I would remember for the rest of my life.

On my own.

After Lily died I spent the rest of that year at home, alone, lonely, and probably depressed although I didn't know it then. My few friends and colleagues — all my friends were colleagues although not all my colleagues were friends — got on with their lives, as people do and must. Lisa was helpless for most of that time, needing more support than anyone could give including Colin, her unsympathetic and impatient fiancé. Doris (and Ngaire) tried hard to help me with both emotional and practical support but, as I have said, they soon withdrew in the face of my admittedly ungracious rejection.

Now I can't remember exactly what I did during all the hours, days, weeks and months of that year. Probably very little. I had few callers or phone calls, and Lily's popularity with the neighbours obviously didn't extend to me; apparently I was considered stand-offish and sometimes downright rude. Doris told me later that most of my neighbours had always felt sorry for Lily and the children and were not surprised that 'the boy' now lived in America and 'the girl' visited only rarely.

Sad and bored — dressed only in shorts and a T-shirt, or perhaps a comfy track suit, frequently unshaven — I found I looked forward to the weekly visit of Ernie and Beth, Lily's gardeners, and the twice-weekly but now hardly-necessary visit of the Russian cleaners (a father, mother and daughter, also Lily's appointees). I kept them on for sentimental reasons and often wasted their time with idle and not always welcome chats. Otherwise, if I remember right, I got up late, watched daytime television, snacked too much, prepared unnecessarily elaborate meals (which consumed a lot of time but which served merely to complement my favourite Burgundy), and, at night, before bed, drank too much *Maker's Mark* which I had learned to like in America.

Although Lisa said she would *never* get over Lily's death she was sufficiently recovered by Christmas to host me and Doris (and Ngaire) — Grace was indisposed by then — to a Christmas dinner at her new Parnell flat which she shared with her by-then reconciled fiancé. I did my best to be jolly but it was a dreary lunch, lacking any festive spirit; I was glad when it was over.

A summer alone and lonely.

I spent that summer at home, alone, lacking even the company of the gardeners and cleaners who were taking their own summer holidays. Idling away the long summer days, lounging beside the pool, eating and drinking too much, I remembered how much Lily and the children loved their camping holidays at Taipa. But, Lil, I used to insist, we could go anywhere. Hawaii, Gold Coast, Fiji, Raro, New Caledonia, Tahiti. Stay at the best hotels. The kids'd love it. But they really *love* camping at Taipa, insisted Lily. So I'd go with them, set up the tent and stay a couple of days. Before long, though, anxious about what was happening in the office, I'd head home, returning only when it was time for the children to go back to school.

During that long and lonely summer I'd have done anything to be back camping at Taipa with Lily and the children. Sometimes — lying alone on a lounger beside the pool — I'd actually curse aloud with what? Grief? Anger? Frustration? I don't know. Shit! I'd shout to the blue sky for some reason. Shit, shit, shit!

At last: the inevitable. On my sixtieth birthday.

Late in April I received a call from Tom Wolfendale. Tom wanted a meeting; not in the office but at my place in Minehaha. We met late the following Monday afternoon, coincidentally my birthday. I had the cleaners in the house but it was a fine day so we sat outside, on the deck, by the pool, looking out over the park-like lawns and gardens still immaculately groomed and maintained by Lily's old gardeners. There, over coffee, made and served by the beautiful young Russian daughter who had taken a liking to me — or taken pity on me — Tom told me of a development that was inevitable.

According to his diplomatic telling, my long absences, because of Lily's illness, especially over the last two years, had shown that the agency could function without me, and this, together with my age — You know, it's a young man's business now, said Tom — and the fact that there was now nothing to stop American ownership of a New Zealand advertising agency, New York wanted to buy me out and take complete ownership of what would then become Ayer New Zealand.

Ayer's terms, later confirmed in writing, were generous. I was impressed and, it must be said, secretly relieved. However, what Tom and I didn't know, and couldn't have guessed, was that all was not well at Ayer in New York and that I was lucky to be offered such a good price.

Anyway, after no more than a few minutes thought, I agreed to Ayer's terms knowing I could trust Tom to follow through with the details. We shook hands without referring to the past, to the many years we had known each other and worked together. Tom left, without ceremony or delay, while I, unwilling to make small talk with the cleaners, stepped down to the lawn. I'll wait till they're gone, I thought, referring to the cleaning family, and then I'll have tea and go for a walk down to the beach for a quiet birthday think.

At dusk I was standing at the bottom of Minehaha gazing across the still and steely-grey sea at Rangitoto while harmless little ripples sloshed and swirled lazily around the rocks at my feet. It was a bit chilly but I didn't mind; I had a warm jacket on, and I needed to think.

Not counting the Russians I had seen only one person all day: Tom Wolfendale with his fateful news. Tom had no reason to know or remember my sixtieth birthday and I didn't mention it.

Alone — alone but not lonely, and strangely content — having thought all my thoughts, I turned for the short walk home, through the chill air, to my empty house having realized, there on the shore, that thanks to N. W. Ayer of New York, I was about to start a new life.

I had no choice really, but I didn't mind. I was thoroughly sick of the old me. It was, I thought, without doubt, time for a change.

9

Now what?

In the quiet and lonely Easter weekend after my Tom Wolfendale meeting I had to face the fact that, at sixty years old, I had just agreed to sell the business which had been my life's work.

Being sixty didn't feel a lot different from being fifty but I knew many men of my generation who were already dead and many more, while still alive, who looked and acted years older as they boringly complained of the number, variety, strength and side-effects of the pills and potions they must take daily to manage their myriad aches, pains and mysterious conditions. I had no such complaints. I was perfectly healthy. And I was rich. But I was also widowed, unemployed, friendless and not entirely happy.

I couldn't help thinking: Now what?

It was eight months since Lily's death and I had achieved nothing. In fact, less than nothing; my affairs were in reverse. I was not only out of my own agency — altogether out of the advertising business — but had also neglected my other affairs: my cash investments and share portfolio, my land investments in Brown's Bay, the Kaukapakapa and Silverdale farms, the Albany and

Rosedale orchards I had bought from Bill Brown, and my Wiri and Wairau Valley commercial tenants, sixteen successful businesses, all making money, paying rent regularly and — good on them — making no demands.

I got on well with my tenants and farm managers and was grateful to them for leaving me alone over those last few months. But as I was 'back in business' I was anxious to catch up, to bring my financial affairs up to date. So I decided to do two things.

First, as I would lose my agency-supplied car I decided to buy something practical and versatile; something big, tough and strong with plenty of carrying capacity at the back and as comfortable as a car inside. In in a word: a ute. At Lyon Motors I took the only one immediately available; a new nineteen eighty-six Ford Falcon, red, manual.

Next, I set up an office in Lily's personal living room-cum-study. I bought a desk and office chair, a portable typewriter and a steel filing cabinet which I filled with the investment files held in my agency office and brought to me by Duane Latrobe's new secretary. She came by taxi so she could drive my agency-supplied Fairmont back to the office.

It took just two weeks to get my affairs in order and catch up with my commercial tenants. But then, after a busy couple of weeks, which I thoroughly enjoyed, I was idle again which I definitely didn't enjoy. I called in to the Auckland Club but couldn't reconnect with anyone there; I no longer shared the members' preoccupations. I resigned from the Rotary Club, declining to transfer my membership to Takapuna, while my Chamber of Commerce membership lapsed with my resignation from the agency.

At last: altogether out of the advertising business.

Ayer settled at the end of June. The formalities were simple and brief: I was required to meet Tom Wolfendale, now acting for Ayer, and Reece Williams — still my lawyer — at the Wolfendale Mills office which was still on the ground floor of the building the part-ownership of which I was about to pass to Ayer New Zealand. Signatures and witnesses were required and that was that; all over in minutes. Tom and I shook hands again and, with Tom's permission, I stopped in at Lisa's office.

Oh, daddy, said a busy-looking Lisa, it's just so frantic around here with this new GST starting in October. Our clients don't know what to do. We're having to run seminars. I'm out every night. Poor Colin. How is he? I asked, trying to be interested and polite. Colin? Well, he's a bit sick of it actually, said Lisa. But what can I do? Well, I'm glad I'm out of it all, I said which wasn't entirely true. But, daddy, said Lisa, you won't escape GST. It'll be everywhere. On everything. For everyone. Really? I said. I was surprised. I hadn't taken much notice of this new Labour government development.

Oh, and by the way, said Lisa leaning back in her chair and fiddling with a pencil. I thought she looked absurdly young to be an accountant advising people like me about their financial affairs. We've set the date, she said. What date? I asked naively. Me and Colin. We're getting married. Easter next year. You'll be father of the bride. I half-smiled, ruefully, but Lisa misunderstood the source of my pain. Poor mum, eh, she said.

While we were chatting much more than a million dollars had passed into my bank account.

Lisa gets married.

Lisa Marie Purvis became Lisa Marie Watt — Mrs Colin

Watt — on the afternoon of Easter Saturday, nineteen eighty-seven, just three days before my sixty-first birthday. The venue was the Anglican church in Killarney Street where I dutifully gave away my daughter (as they say), walking her up the aisle to her waiting fiancé, thinking only that, tall and blonde, she was at least as elegant and beautiful as her mother, especially in her wedding gown, and that I was delivering her into the care of a stupid and undeserving young oaf who didn't deserve her and wouldn't care for her as he should and she deserved.

As we waited anxiously together in the church porch, Lisa's arm linked through mine, with one bridesmaid, Tui Parāone, behind us for company, I turned to my beautiful daughter and whispered: Lisa, darling... to which she looked momentarily angry, scowling, and said sharply — as if she knew what I was going to say — No, daddy! Not now. It's too late.

At the reception, at the Romaleigh in Northcote, I met the groom's parents for the first and only time. It was a lavish affair, planned by Lisa and paid for by me, at which Colin, in his speech, made inappropriate remarks about Tui, his best man told an obscene and utterly irrelevant joke about what may or may not be lurking under a Scotsman's kilt, and Mr Watt senior got drunk — Never seen so much free food and piss in all me life, he said — and passed out, to the disgust of his wife, as Lisa and her somewhat intoxicated groom stood up to attempt their first dance as man and wife.

I tried to be tolerant of the groom and his family but Doris (and Ngaire) were blunt. Men! said Ngaire in disgust. It'll never last, Eddie, said Doris. You do know that, don't you? I merely nodded grimly.

A fresh start in a new apartment.

Takapuna was changing. After just two years there was much Lily wouldn't recognize. Many of her favourite little owner-operated shops were gone, or going, and many of the old houses, especially those near the beach, were being bought by developers to be replaced by modern apartments. That brought new residents who drove the demand for restaurants, cafes and bars. Takapuna was no longer the sleepy seaside suburb it was when Lily and I moved there in nineteen sixty.

I was sentimentally attached to Minehaha but was beginning to see what many others saw and were saying: that it was ridiculous for one man in his sixties to live alone in a large family home on a huge double section. I was beginning to tire of the effort, for the sake of Lily's memory, when a beachside building of luxury apartments, with panoramic views across the gulf to Rangitoto, was opened on my virtual doorstep; all I had to do was choose one.

Minehaha sold quickly, much to my relief and Lisa's dismay. Lisa cried when I told her of my plans to sell and move; she cried again as she helped me dispose of Lily's clothes and make-up and personal items. However, I kept Lily's jewellery, her favourite books, LPs and CDs. I also kept most of her paintings as I knew how valuable they were and how good they'd look in my new apartment.

Lisa cried again when the hammer came down at the Barfoot auction rooms; I had to comfort her there, awkwardly, in public, before receiving the auctioneer's congratulations. I'll have to tell John, she said. I wrote to him, I said. Told him what was happening. He wasn't worried. Wasn't he? Lisa was surprised. Well, I'll email him anyway. Tell him it's all over. If you like, I said.

I asked Lisa then if she would help me get an email address. I need to get completely sorted on the computer, I said, knowing I had no choice; I had to join the computer age.

I quickly settled into my three-bedroom penthouse apartment which, in its own way, was as ridiculously large for one man in his sixties living alone as Minehaha had been. But I enjoyed its modernity, the grand views from its balcony, and the freedom it gave me from land and building maintenance. I rehired the Russian housekeepers to do a once-weekly quick and easy clean as well as my laundry and ironing. They liked it — as I did — that everything was new including the latest appliances. All the furniture was new too.

I took nothing from Minehaha except Lily's art and I enjoyed it when my interior decorating consultant Beverly Something gasped — literally gasped, with wide open mouth and eyes — when Lily's paintings were uncrated for hanging. With that she confirmed what I knew: Lily had impeccable taste in art, as in everything.

It was later that that year, nineteen eighty-seven, that Grace died horribly —and with inconsiderate cruelty as far as Lisa and I were concerned — on Lily's second anniversary. There was no funeral, there was no one to mourn 'the poor woman', as Doris referred to her. But Ngaire, always staunch and reliable, apparently arranged everything: that is, dealing with the police and coroner and arranging an after-hours cremation.

Introducing Minta.

I was pretty good on my computer by then, and had mastered email, so I was able to communicate quickly, easily and often with John in America. John — who hated letter writing and long-distance telephone calls — also found emailing easy. The two of us reestablished a line of communication which had become frayed since John moved to America. I found it easier — easier than speaking face-to-face — to tell John, and copy Lisa and Doris (and Ngaire), that Grace had died, and how, although they all knew why.

John replied then — to all — with the news that he had been married for a month to a girl he had been dating since he arrived in America in nineteen eighty-four. Her name, he said, was Minta Tilson Quilly. She's a physicist, he wrote, working in a team, at another university, in a joint project with Cambridge University in England and a famous young physicist there called Stephen Hawking.

Lisa's miscarriage.

Late the following year Lisa had a miscarriage. I wouldn't have known except a broken-hearted (and briefly hospitalized) Lisa confided in her Aunt Doris (and Ngaire) who told me although only when the patient had recovered and was settled at home. I learned later that the naturally kind Doris and the fiercely practical Ngaire had combined to give Lisa the female emotional support she might otherwise have received from her mother.

I was awkwardly embarrassed to learn from my sister about my daughter's miscarriage. I didn't even like to think about my lovely Lisa — so like her mother in so many ways — doing 'it' with the flabby and overweight young Colin, let alone the sad and intimate details of a miscarriage. I didn't even know she was having a baby, I said. It was early days, said Doris. Nobody knew. Not even Colin. But it's still an awful thing for a woman.

Introducing Maggie.

I wouldn't have known what to do, how to react, if not

for my new lady friend Margaret who encouraged me to send flowers first and then arrange a quiet visit during the day. When she's on her own, she said. It'll be easier to have a quiet dad-to-daughter chat.

But what about you know who and what? I asked, referring to my contempt for Lisa's useless husband and my desire to buy her a house. He'll never be able to afford anything decent. That's not for now, insisted Margaret. I don't know Lisa but I *do* know she'll be in a fragile emotional state. She doesn't need her rich father to go blundering in with ridiculous suggestions that imply God-knows-what about her husband. But he's such a useless prick, I said. None of your business, said sensible down-to-earth Margaret.

In the three years since Lily's death I had not gone entirely without female company. But what I didn't seek — didn't want — was any physical intimacy. Most if not all my companions were pleased with this non-demand which meant they were universally disappointed to learn that any further commitment from me, more than an occasional outing, was out of the question. But Margaret Mary Carrucan — everyone called her Maggie — was different. She didn't need or seek male companionship. Even when male company would have made a social event more pleasant she happily — confidently — attended on her own, mixing with the cream of Auckland's business, political and social elite, posing for photographs, always wearing a glamorous new gown and her favourite jewellery.

Margaret was a wealthy woman — not as wealthy as I but wealthy enough — having not only been born into money but later marrying a young man who made a fortune digging drains and laying concrete until he died from nothing worse than hard work.

I knew her through Rotary. I ran into her again at an

Accountants' Society dinner. Lisa was there to receive an award and I was acting as her consort as Colin was unable — unwilling I thought — to attend. That gorgeous young thing, said Margaret, teasingly, when we met at the bar after dinner. Young enough to be your daughter. She *is* my daughter, I said. I should have guessed, said Margaret. So like Lily. She's Lisa, I said. Oh, little Lisa, said Margaret. Lisa Watt now, I said. Mrs Watt. Oh, I see, said Margaret ambivalently.

Without making a commitment, or worrying about motives, Margaret and I became a comfortable couple. One thing puzzled Margaret though and she asked me about it. I thought wildly ambitious and successful men were supposed to have a huge sex drive, she said. I know Leo did. It's all the testosterone. It drives them. But not you, Eddie. Not you. So what happened?

What drove me, I know now, I said, was the fear of poverty. I hated it, you know. When I was a kid. I hated being poor. I hated my father for losing his job and being an alcoholic. And my poor mother for putting up with him. Never having enough money. All that. That's what drove me. Apart from that, Lily was everything. I didn't need anyone else. Still don't if you know what I mean. No offence.

I know what you mean, said Margaret. Me and Leo. He was a wonderful husband. Well, actually, I said, to tell you the truth, Lily was a wonderful wife but I was a pretty shit husband.

Doris (and Ngaire) return.

Time passed quickly then as it does for those growing old. Days folded into weeks, weeks into months until, suddenly, it was September nineteen eighty-nine. One cool evening I was sitting, on my sheltered balcony, watching wind surfers skidding across the green and choppy waters off Takapuna beach, wishing for spring, thinking about getting ready for Margaret's fifty-sixth birthday dinner. It felt nice to be soon going out for a pleasant evening with a kind and intelligent woman who had lately become my almost constant companion.

That's probably her now, I thought when I heard the phone ringing inside. But it wasn't Margaret, it was Doris. Dossy, I said, pleased to be hearing from my older sister; despite our occasional disagreement, and my casual attitude, we were still mildly fond of each. Long time no hear, I said brightly. Well, we're back, said Doris. Back? I was puzzled. Back from where? I asked.

I tried to explain it to Margaret later, at dinner, although it was hard when we were sharing a table with guests. She said I knew, I said. She said she told me months ago. Even sent me postcards, which I never received by the way. They take ages, said Margaret. Anyway, where did they go? That's the thing, I said. I can't believe she told me. I would have remembered that. Remembered what? asked Margaret. Well, they've been to Germany to meet our mother's family. So many relations. She told me the place but I can't remember. Something German sounding. Well, it would be, wouldn't it, said Margaret. I ignored the sarcasm and continued. Said she learned German. Been learning it properly for years she said. I didn't know *that*. And now she wants to tell me all about it, show me all the photos. I can't believe it. Germany. All that time and I didn't even know she was gone.

Margaret had never met Doris (and Ngaire) and they didn't know she existed nor of the fondness between us which must have been obvious when they did meet. That was at my place on the Sunday afternoon following Margaret's Thursday-night birthday dinner. Ngaire had assembled all the trip photos in date order, captioned with names, dates and places, in a fat red plastic-covered photo album through which she and Doris guided the still-astonished but somewhat bored me and the more attentive and interested Margaret. They sat on one of my bigger couches, Margaret and me together flanked by Doris and Ngaire.

Well, said Doris to begin, this is us at the airport leaving for Singapore. We had two nights there. What a wonderful place, said Ngaire. So clean and organized. Anyway, mustn't linger there, said Doris who was anxious to get to family matters. What an amazing airport, continued Ngaire. We were heading for Frankfurt, see, said Doris. I tried to be interested in Singapore and its 'amazing' airport, and Frankfurt, but wasn't; I had been to both many times. Margaret, too, was well travelled but managed to show more interest.

I did get mildly interested when they reached the family photos. This is mama's only brother left of the five of them. It's our Uncle Klaus, Eddie. I stared at an obviously old and German-looking man wearing rimless spectacles. He had a round and ruddy face, thick lips, a big nose, a bush of white hair. I tried — looked hard — but couldn't see any resemblance to mother. Nor did he look especially athletic. He's seventy-nine years old, protested Doris. What do you expect? Anyway they're not acrobats anymore. Not in the circus or anything. But, Eddie, look at him, continued Doris. Our only remaining uncle in all the world.

I'd never thought of having a German uncle; the only uncle I ever knew — ever thought of, even now — was my father's brother, Tobias, my generous Uncle Toby.

There was more; page after turned page of German relatives, young and old, teenagers and babies. All grinning madly at the camera. All looking like people anywhere. They posed in the summer sun, in the garden of someone's house, around a dinner table somewhere, in a *Biergarten* or *Gasthaus*.

And that's not all of them, said Doris as she closed the heavy album. There's heaps more but they live all over the place. Some stayed in Switzerland after the war. But most are now in Erding. That's where we were.

Think of it, Eddie. Mama would be a great-great-great aunt to all the German babies. Even old Uncle Klaus, the youngest of mama's siblings — he only speaks German — he has many great grandchildren. And a couple of great-great grandchildren I think, added Ngaire.

So how did you get on with talking? I asked. Oh, most of the young ones speak perfect English, said Doris. Germans do, you know. But my German's always been good. Better than yours, that's for sure. But it's even better now. We stayed with mama's family all the time. Speaking proper German to everyone. It was marvellous. It really was. You should have been there, Eddie.

Where was this place, anyway? I asked. It's called Erding, said Doris. A lovely little town near Munich. *München*. In Bavaria. It's the beer capital of Germany, said Ngaire rubbing her hands together at the thought of foaming Erding beer served in tall glasses by costumed *junge Männer und Frauen*. I had seen the photos. Really, she added, *das beste bier der welt*.

You *really* don't want to go to Germany to meet all your relatives? asked Margaret later that Sunday night. Not really, I said. Haven't you got any other family? asked Margaret. Only one cousin, I said. My Uncle Toby and Aunt Edith had just one kid. David. A bit older than me. A proper bloody snob. What does he do? She asked. Some sort of language expert, I said. Actually I think he teaches German. Does he have any children? I don't know, I said. He's married but I'm pretty sure he's gay. Well you've got that big family in Germany, said Margaret. I'm surprised you don't want to go and visit them.

If I go anywhere, I said, I'll go and see John in America.

10

John and Minta in America.

Exactly a year later, in what Americans call 'the fall', I found myself shaking hands with my tall, dark, handsome and fit-and-healthy-looking son in the arrivals hall of the huge Hartsfield International Airport in Atlanta, Georgia. Despite my experience and travels with Pan Am I'd never been to Atlanta — never been anywhere in America's south except for one family visit to Washington, DC — and after only a few years of non-travel I felt like a novice.

I had considered going on to New York and Germany but was glad I hadn't. I decided there was no one I wanted to see in New York anymore, nothing I wanted to do there that I hadn't done. Same with Germany: I had been there many times — mostly to Frankfurt — and had no desire to return. And, despite the enthusiastic urging of Doris (and Ngaire), I still had no desire to meet my German relatives.

I wished Margaret had come but she'd insisted. It's nothing to do with me, she said. After all that's happened you need time with your son. And you've never even met your daughter-in-law.

Minta couldn't make it, said John as we walked out of

the big noisy terminal. But she'll be home tonight. We're going to the (John said a posh-sounding name I can't remember) Club for dinner. He had a big American car — an impressive Lincoln Continental — which he drove expertly and sedately on one busy freeway after another, until we arrived at the (Something) Plantation (I never could remember the name of that place), a gated estate where he and Minta owned a condominium at least as large and spacious as Minehaha. And they don't even have kids, I said to Margaret later.

I had my own bedroom and bathroom there, and was left to look after myself for most of my two-and-a-half week stay. Minta gave me the use of her car — a little Saab — saying she could easily manage without it; John could give her a ride to work. I discovered later that that wasn't entirely true; although Minta and John had met at John's university Minta had since moved on to another, still in Atlanta, so she probably needed her car. It was the first hint I had of her kind and generous nature.

Atlanta and the American civil war.

With the help of a road atlas, a tourist guide book, some suggestions from Minta, and the use of her car, I used my time alone, all day, Monday to Friday, to see the sights. I quickly learned that, apart from being the home of Coca Cola, three things dominated Atlanta tourism: the civil war, the movie *Gone With The Wind* which was *about* the civil war, and the civil rights movement which was in effect an *extension* of the civil war. It was all interesting but being a solo tourist was depressing; the desire to share what I saw, to observe and comment, to discuss over coffee or lunch, was almost overwhelming. But I soldiered on thinking constantly that everything I saw and learned would have been more enjoyable in

Lily's company (or Margaret's or John and Minta's for that matter, but especially Lily's) and would have meant more to Lily whose seeing and learning would be enhanced by what she already knew of the civil war, *Gone With The Wind* and the American civil rights movement.

I knew Lily would have been enchanted to go shopping, as I did, at the Peachtree Battle shopping centre; it was named for Peachtree Battle Avenue which was itself named for the civil war Battle of Peachtree Creek. It was there, incidentally, while browsing in a book store, that I picked up an *Advertising Age* — I hadn't seen one for years — and learned, for the first time, that Pan Am was in financial trouble. I wondered, naturally, how that was affecting the agency in New York and around the world, including New Zealand. I bought the *Advertising Age*, meaning to read it later, but found I was no longer interested in the details and politics of the industry which had been my life's work.

I enjoyed my visit to the famous Atlanta Cyclorama, a circular diorama of the famous Battle of Atlanta in July, eighteen sixty-four, which was the background for *Gone With The Wind*. I remembered how much Lily had liked the movie, especially Vivien Leigh's performance as Scarlett O'Hara. I was quietly amused therefore when the narrator pointed to one particular confederate soldier — a uniformed mannequin lying 'dead' in the foreground — and explained that it was a late addition. Evidently when Clark Gable, who played Rhett Butler in the film, visited the Cyclorama after the world premier of *Gone With The Wind*, at the Fox theatre in Atlanta, he said it was okay — pretty good, he said — but there was one thing wrong. The problem is, he said, *I'm* not in it. And so they added that dead soldier with a thin moustache, to represent the famous actor.

I smiled then but knew that Lily would have laughed

out loud, remembered the story and then, once home, would have told everyone what she knew about the famous Clark Gable.

I knew, with equal certainty, that she would have been heart-broken — moved to silent tears — if she could have seen what I saw on the day I dedicated to Martin Luther King, Jr. I was surprised to be so moved myself when I visited his birth home followed by a visit to the Ebenezer Baptist church — where King had been a pastor until his assassination — and the nearby Martin Luther King memorial. For the first time I was glad, in a strange way, that Lily was *not* with me; surely, I thought, she would have been emotionally drained by the experience of that day.

The protesting Minta.

At dinner that night Minta was especially interested in my day. She was only ten years old when King was assassinated but she was intimately familiar with the civil rights issue in the South, particularly in rural Georgia where she grew up, having experienced racial prejudice and discrimination as a child, even at school. It wasn't too bad at college, she said, but as a little 'coloured' girl at school — my father was black you see, a 'negro' then — the white children could be cruel.

But! I protested impulsively, awkwardly; then I didn't know what to say next. Kind Minta rescued me; saved me from my foot-in-mouth self. I know, she said emphatically. Y'all look at me and I know what you think. Well, they called me the 'lucky one'. Y'all should see my sister. Black! Oh my God, father-in-law. That girl!

I was relieved and grateful.

There was no legal segregation then, she continued, not real laws. Not in our town anyway, she said. But all the same we coloured kids had separate bathrooms and ate our lunches separately. Had to sit apart at the movies. Even on some of the buses an' all. I didn't protest then. I suppose I didn't know any better — my parents just accepted those things, you know — but I'm ashamed now, I really am.

Which is why she was so active in college, interrupted John who had been silent, listening, until then. She got arrested three times, he said. I did, said Minta, and you know what-all, father-in-law? — she touched my arm gently, intimately — I'm goddamn proud of it. And she said it all in a soft southern accent which I found charming but which I knew belied the intelligence, education and steely determination I sensed in my newly-met daughter-in-law.

Food.

We were at a lobster restaurant, where the food was delicious but the portions were obscenely large. John and Minta devoured their food, with sweet iced tea, and I wondered why they weren't fat. I thought John, an athletics coach, should have been more careful about his diet. But I was getting used to Southern-style American dining where wine was rarely if ever served and most meals were eaten out; and quickly. It seemed that in the South no one lingered over a meal as they did at home and in most places in the world including New York.

Although John and Minta did eat breakfast at home — when John returned and showered after his morning run — it was usually no more than a cup or two of strong and bitter American coffee and, sometimes, a pastry or muffin. But at night I never saw them cook, or the fully-equipped kitchen used for anything but making coffee or microwaving something from a box.

I thought Lily would be horrified.

John, the university track and field coach.
In the eighteen days of my stay we ate at home only twice. Even then John and Minta didn't cook but ordered huge pizzas over which — with beer — we watched hours-long college football games. Not only was it the only time during my stay that John and Minta ate at home together but it was also the only time during my visit I saw John get excited about anything; on each occasion his university was one of the football teams.

He had played first fifteen for Takapuna Grammar and, later, on the wing for Otago university, where he trialled for Otago, so I couldn't understand how he could get wrapped up in such a strange and drawn-out game.

Minta sensed my confusion. It's *his* college, she said during one of the many breaks when John was taking a break of his own. He's on the coaching staff. I couldn't believe it. Coaching *that?* I asked, pointing to the television screen. Not *football*, said Minta. No. John's track and field. A fitness fanatic actually. But the football coaches, they're all his co-workers. It's big there, sports, at his college. Real big, you know.

I nodded but didn't really understand how important John was to the university's sporting success and reputation. Seeing my doubt, Minta leaned across, touched my arm in the way she had, and said: He's clever, your boy, father-in-law. Real respected as a coach. And a good man. A really *good* man. At which I smiled and nodded with gratitude. His mother would have loved you, I said.

But I thought, despite what Minta had said about him, Lily would have been disappointed in her son.

John asked about Lisa only once, in passing, on the only occasion when we were alone together. It was a weekend trip to the zoo which reminded me of the days, long ago, I spent sketching zoo animals. She's fine, as far as I know, I said. But what about her husband, Colin whatshisname? asked John. I don't really know, I said. He doesn't say much. Or do much. I hardly know him really. I was surprised by John's questions; I had assumed he and Lisa were in constant contact.

Minta came with John to see me off on my long return journey. It was nice to get an affectionate hug, and a kiss on the cheek, from my tall, slim, attractive and evidently very clever daughter-in-law — so highly-respected in international science circles — as she whispered in my ear: Y'all come back one day.

On the other hand I wasn't surprised to get no more than a strong handshake from John, and a direct but inscrutable look in the eye — veiled and cold — from which I was able to deduce nothing. See ya, dad, he said. I'll email. See ya, son, I said. Be in touch. And that was that.

Time to think.

On the journey home, two long flights, I had plenty of time — almost a full day including a wait in Los Angeles — to do what I never used to do but had begun to do often, albeit with limited success: I tried to understand people. In this case John and Minta.

I wondered, between meals and restless dozing: why John had abandoned New Zealand, his mother in particular; how John and Minta had met and why they were so different from each other; if they were they planning to have children and if so whether Minta knew about Lily's inheritable disease; above all, why my own son was so aloof and remote even, as far as I could tell, from his lovely wife. Perhaps he's different with her, in private, I thought. Hoped. Who knows? Who knows anything about the private lives of any couple?

In the end, before I got home, before I had to explain anything to Lisa, Margaret, and Doris (and Ngaire), I decided I was poorly equipped to understand people — not just John and Minta but *people* — and began to wonder about myself. How did people see me then; and before, in business? Was I likeable? I didn't think so. I knew many people found me irritable and short-tempered. Intimidating, Lily used to say. So how, I wondered, had I managed to win such a wonderful wife, and raise two children, and build such a successful business?

And what about Margaret? I suddenly saw that she was doing what Lily must have always done: explaining people to me and me to them. I know she does it, I thought. But why? I realized then, again, how much I owed Lily. I wish I'd thanked her more and decided I would, from the minute I landed and met Margaret waiting at the airport, listen more to *her* about other people and their feelings, take *her* advice and, above all, thank her in the way I never thanked Lily.

Atlanta as a marker.

Before the Atlanta trip I had always remembered events and experiences as occurring before or after Lily. But after the trip — in September nineteen ninety — events and experiences came to be remembered as before or after Atlanta.

The first big event after Atlanta came early in the new year when I learned that Pan Am had filed for bankruptcy and that the New York agency had — obviously — lost the account world-wide. I was relieved to learn, though, that the agency had been appointed by Continental Airlines, there and around the world, and that Ayer New Zealand — in which I now had only a sentimental interest — would not be unduly affected.

Father Time and Mother Nature.

Father Time and Mother Nature conspire to remind even the healthiest and most robust men amongst us that despite their intellect and ego, their success in their chosen field, their wealth and fame, they are all, at base, mere animals comprising a skeletal frame supporting a sack of organs all of which are subject to failure, decay and disease.

I didn't say all that. I remember it as the grim lesson, received by me, delivered with a smile by the young Doctor Eskdale who looked to be about fourteen years old but was an eminently respected GP. He had recently moved to Takapuna to replace Lily's retired doctor. It was on the occasion of my return visit after my annual check-up, when blood tests had revealed the need for precautionary blood-pressure and cholesterol medication.

You mean for the rest of my life? I asked. Yes, said the doctor. The benefits are proven. Otherwise heart attack? Stroke? Death? And we wouldn't want that would we. It wasn't a question. Every day for the rest of my life? I asked again. These therapies are entirely routine for men your age, said the doctor. Ask your friends. You'll see.

He's right, said Margaret. All my brothers and brothers-in-law, those that aren't dead, they're all on those medicines.

Sixty-five and getting the pension, I thought ruefully. Can't believe it.

More benign evidence of Father Time and Mother Nature's corrupting work — evident in the mirror — were my thinning hair being almost entirely grey, and severe facial creases that looked like angry lines of expression but were permanent. Not evident in the mirror but nevertheless real, were occasional breathlessness and a lessening of strength, vigour and stamina which annoyed rather than worried me.

The evidence of aging — medical and visible — was the second unexpected event following my Atlanta trip. But there was more to come.

Lisa's (good) news.

Next, about that time — the middle of nineteen ninety-one — I got a call from Lisa. Daddy, we need to talk, she said. I thought she sounded nervous. When we met — she came to my place after work and we went to dinner at a quiet restaurant in Milford — she wasn't nervous but rather formal and business-like. She gave nothing away while we waited for our wine. But once we'd clinked glasses — she said Cheer's, daddy, with a nervous smile — and she'd blurted out the reason for our meeting, she relaxed visibly and discussed the matter openly, without bitterness, while we enjoyed a leisurely evening together.

Lisa and Colin have split up, I told Margaret the next day. Never seemed like a happy match to me, said Margaret. It wasn't, I said. To me it's just good news. So what happens now? asked Margaret. I don't know, I said. He's gone. Don't know where. But she's staying in the flat. It was always hers anyway and now she's going to buy it. Good on her, said Margaret. She's doing well at Tom's place, I said. A partner soon I think. Can easily afford it now, on her own. I don't how she got mixed up with him but I'm glad it's over. For her sake I mean.

I never saw Colin Watt again and so he must be faded out of my story.

A double tragedy after Atlanta. And more.

Things kept getting worse with a double tragedy in nineteen ninety-three.

First, at the beginning of the year, a very ill Doris was diagnosed with aggressive and incurable pancreatic cancer. She (and Ngaire) had retired and were living in a cottage at Muriwai. Treatment was given, and received with hope, but was painful and ultimately futile.

Doris Sabine Purvis died in July that year aged sixty-nine.

Her awful death — it was painful, and far from peaceful — was followed just two days later by Ngaire's. Why Ngaire chose to end her own life was understandable to any who knew her and Doris, but talking about how she did it would be horrible and would add nothing to my story. Typical of Ngaire though: she had prearranged a joint Doris/Ngaire funeral at the Muriwai surf club.

That double tragedy, which affected me more than I could admit, was followed by news that was sad rather than tragic. But coming from Tom Wolfendale, immediately after Doris (and Ngaire)'s funeral, nevertheless overwhelmed me, forcing me to think more about the past then I ever liked to.

Old Terry passed away yesterday, said Tom. He was referring to Terry Staines, my first proper media manager whom I employed in nineteen fifty-three and who, as an experienced advertising professional, was responsible, amongst other things, for helping turn little Purvis Commercial Art into Purvis Advertising Limited. He had introduced me to Tom — another slick professional — who had guided my financial affairs ever since.

I remembered Terry for his old-fashioned integrity,

his rather dour nature, his impeccable grooming — he always wore a three-piece suit and a smart hat — and his posh English accent, and found it hard and depressing to think of him as a frail ninety-two-year-old, riddled with cancer, dying alone — a childless widower — in a Herne Bay hospice. I should have visited him, I said to Tom. Over the years. I should have. But I never did.

Tom Wolfendale said nothing.

Getting philosophical about death and dying.

Everything's gone wrong since Atlanta, I thought constantly and said once to Margaret. I was thinking of myself, my health, my ageing body, the medication I had to take, the far-away failing of Pan Am and its as yet unknown long-term affect on Ayer, of the poor relationship I had with John — I'd hardly heard from him since Atlanta — and of Lisa's failed marriage.

And that's not all, I said. You mean Doris and Ngaire? asked Margaret. Exactly, I said but I was also thinking of Terry Staines. But she was sixty-nine, Eddie, said Margaret. It's sad, I know, but she and you, and me for that matter, it's our age. Things start going wrong. Our bodies start failing.

Father Time and Mother Nature, I said, recalling the words of young Doctor Eskdale, but Margaret only nodded. When I was young, I said, I thought only old people died. But we *are* old people, Eddie, said Margaret. It's *our* turn. Somehow — at that moment but not for the first time — she seemed wiser than I.

Margaret was right of course. Over the next few years I was always hearing about someone my age or younger becoming ill and dying of this or that, or dying suddenly, without warning. I realized that many if not most or all the people older than me whom I had met in business over the years — people in the agency, in New York, around the world, clients, suppliers and professionals, members of the Auckland Club, the chamber of commerce and Parnell Rotary — were probably all dead or dying.

The bad news continued. I heard from Lisa, who had heard it from a university friend of a friend, that my only New Zealand cousin David Purvis — Uncle Toby's snobby son — had collapsed and died suddenly in the Victoria University cafeteria. Was he still working? I asked Lisa. Why shouldn't he be? asked Lisa. You are.

Running my land holdings — I was planning then to subdivide and sell all my land — didn't seem like work to me.

And then I learned, also from Lisa, that Penny Brown — Peni Parāone — had died at home in Dargaville. Lisa heard it from the Browns' daughter Tui, her bridesmaid, who was a nurse at Auckland hospital. Next I heard, this time from Tom Wolfendale, that my very clever QC Reece Williams had died in a care home in Remuera, his once-active and clever mind afflicted by severe dementia.

Introducing Ross Tayloe and Purvis Developments.

I had decided to subdivide all my land holdings in Rosedale and Brown's Bay, and elsewhere in the booming north and west of the North Shore; a long process.

I used one of my units in Porana Road as a base, and hired a young, enthusiastic and eminently qualified quantity surveyor — his name was Ross Tayloe but he was commonly known as Rosco — to superintend what was to become a years-long project. I liked Ross at our first meeting, and time only confirmed my first impression. He soon proved his worth being experienced in more than his own discipline: diplomatic, intelligent, conscientious, reliable, honest and trustworthy.

As part of his employment I turned over my (second) Ford ute to him which left me carless. To hell with it, I said to Margaret. I'm nearly seventy years old, I've always wanted a sports car — which wasn't true — so I'm going to get one while I can still get in and out of it. Good on you, Eddie, she said. I chose a new 1996 Mazda MX-6 convertible but I had to wait a couple of weeks for the colour I wanted.

I couldn't sleep that night. I had just bought a snazzy little sports car and yet my mind was involuntarily occupied with thoughts of death. I was listing, in random order, as their names occurred to me, all the people who were once part of my life but were now known to be (or almost certainly were) dead including: Lily, her (real) mother Grace, Grace's mother (Lily's real grandmother), my own father and mother, Catherine-Ann, Uncle Toby, Aunt Edith and cousin David, Doris (and Ngaire), Penny Brown — God, I thought, I wish I'd never lost touch with Willy — Reece Williams (my very clever lawyer), Bill and Barry Williams (my first employers but no relation to Reece), the important people from my art studio days including Irma-Leigh Colherne and Morris John, Joyce Ronayne (my first girlfriend), Barbara Ormeskirke (from Milne & Choyce) and her boss Mr Hines, Terry Staines, and all the Ayer people in New York and around the world.

How can it be, I puzzled in my confused and disturbed sleeplessness, that all those people, who were once living, who all had hopes and worries and jobs and mortgages and parents and relatives and children and friends and homes and cars and clothes and pets and hobbies, how can it that they are simply no more? They all died, and the world I'm alive in now — having foolishly just bought a new sports car — carries on as if they never existed.

So what about me? No grandchildren. Will I ever be a grandfather? John and Minta didn't seem inclined. And now poor Lisa, her useless husband and unhappy childless marriage; will she meet someone else? Will she ever have children? What is she now? Thirty-four or something. Possible. But what about Lily's 'thing'?

Thinking of Lisa I fell asleep at last remembering only that she and Margaret thought I should do something for my seventieth birthday in, what? just a couple of weeks. Me. Seventy, I thought. Where the hell did that time go?

The next morning, tired and depressed after such a disturbed and restless night, I remembered I had to pick up my new car. I thought then: What the hell am I doing? I'm nearly seventy, and a new sports car. I'm an idiot.

Later that morning I heard from Tom Wolfendale that Duane Latrobe — I still thought of him as young Duane — had died in his sleep from what was later determined to be a brain aneurism. That was in nineteen ninety-six when he, like me, was almost seventy years old.

11

A seventieth birthday of surprises.

Despite having had plenty of birthdays I've never cared for celebrations. I always thought children's birthdays were worth celebrating because — in the past at least — so many children died young. For a child to have survived another year was worth a celebration. But to me, especially in my dreary old age, every adult birthday just marked another year nearer death. Why celebrate that?

By the time I was seventy I could see there was no beginning or end to the parade of sick and dying people. I knew I was rare in my generation: I was *alive*.

Only under extreme pressure from Lisa and Margaret I reluctantly agreed to a small seventieth birthday dinner. They had arranged a private room at a favourite little Italian restaurant in Jervois Road. They didn't know it but it reminded me of the wonderful times Lily and I had in Italy.

I was surprised, when we arrived, to find a table set for seven. I counted the places and looked at Margaret with raised eyebrows. Lisa's bringing a friend, she said quietly, making little finger quote marks in the air as she said 'friend'. I was intrigued; I could see there must also be *other* unknown guests but, willing to be surprised, I didn't press Margaret further. It turned out to be a night of surprises.

Lisa's two surprises.

The first surprise was Lisa's 'friend'. You know Rosco don't you, daddy. I certainly do, I said — surprised but not unpleased — as I shook hands vigorously with my employee. Mr Purvis, said Ross Tayloe nervously. Eddie! I said heartily, wanting to show my approval to Lisa who, standing at Ross's side, was also looking a bit nervous. Call me Eddie. From now on. I mean it.

I knew, as I said it, that things could become awkward for us both; and for Lisa. Somehow, though, I had a good feeling about Ross and the future. Well, call me Rosco, said Ross with a smiling reply.

My old friend and accountant, Tom Wolfendale, arrived next. He was retired from the firm but was still a partner or something. We had been in business together, one way or another, since nineteen fifty-three when Tom and his partner Frank Mills moved into the house at the other end of the Symonds Street terrace from Purvis Commercial Art; after forty-three years we were still good mates. Tom apologized for his wife's absence although I knew that Dilys Wolfendale, a noted Auckland socialite who had never liked me — had publicly, often, shown her contempt for me — was now confined to a care home with Alzheimer's disease. I felt sorry for Tom and guilty for being a bit glad about his unpleasant wife's misfortune.

Tom's arrival prompted Lisa to surprise me, again, with the news that she had been appointed a partner, the first female partner, of Wolfendale Mills, to which Tom Wolfendale nodded smilingly with approval. I, too, smiled with pride and left my place at the table to give

Lisa a kiss on the cheek. It was then I saw that she and Ross were holding hands under the table and that the young man seemed as pleased and proud of Lisa as I was.

The biggest surprise.
The biggest surprise was the arrival of Willy Parāone although I now thought of him only as Bill Brown. I stood up to greet my old — old in both senses of the word — friend.

You look bloody good for your age, boy, he said, standing back, after our vigorous hand-shaking, to inspect *his* old — in both senses of the word — friend. And so do you, I replied. And we were both telling the truth.

I noticed a young woman standing with Bill but chose to ignore her for the moment. Oh, but I'm so sorry about Penny, I said. So bloody sorry. Thank you, said Bill. I got your card. But Lily too. They were girlfriends, eh. I got your card, from Penny and you, I said. Kept it actually. So what is it now? I asked about Penny. Nearly eighteen months, said Bill. Lily's gone nearly eleven years, I said. Terrible, eh, said Bill.

So how come you're here? I asked. Bill quicky turned to his young woman companion and said, simply: Tui. The young woman smiled shyly and said Tēnā koe, Mr Purvis, and I remembered. Lisa's bridesmaid, I said. Tui nodded across the table to Lisa and said: Me and Lisa are still friends you know. I *do* know that, I said. Actually, I'd forgotten.

Did you hear from John today? Lisa asked as we were leaving the restaurant. I shook my head slowly. I reminded him, said Lisa with a shrug. Never mind, love, I said.

Life after seventy.

After that — my seventieth birthday — life slowed down a lot. I was still the same tall and straight Eddie Purvis although my hair was now real thin and entirely white. And the spectacles, which had first been prescribed when I was in my late fifties, were now thicker and permanent; and at the temple tips, hidden behind my white hair, were fine wires leading to tiny hearing-aid buds in my ears.

Margaret, younger than me, was aging in her own womanly way. She had become what used to be called 'buxom'. Her naturally wavy hair was now kept short, and was streaked with steely grey, but her frequent eyes-and-mouth smile was still broad and sincere. She was always kind to *all* people; I never knew how she did that.

Yet despite her warm and loving nature, which I have to admit brought out the best in me, and the increasing closeness, we still lived apart. She had sold the Devonport house, which she and her Leo had shared for so long, and had bought an apartment in Killarney Street. We agreed that while we enjoyed each other's company we also treasured our independence.

Purvis Developments six years later.

Ross had been managing the Purvis Developments' subdivisions and the progressive sale of our sections. It was an enormous project including all my early land investments in what was by then a very suburban Brown's Bay, the Kaukapakapa and Silverdale farms, as well as the large Albany and Rosedale orchards I'd bought from the departing Bill Brown in nineteen seventy-eight. Ross reported to me regularly while Lisa, as a partner in Wolfendale Mills, was intimately involved in the entire process.

Finally, early in the summer of two thousand and one,

after more than six years work, at enormous cost, the last of the Purvis Developments' sections was sold. As a result there were hundreds of new and happy section owners, dozens of richer real estate agents, and hundreds of carpenters and tradesmen contracted to build all the new houses with consequential flow-on benefits to local furnishing and appliance retailers.

When it was over Ross was physically and emotionally exhausted but exceedingly satisfied. He was grateful, too, for the big bonus I gave him together with the promise of continued employment managing my growing portfolio of commercial properties. Lisa — still Lisa Watt but divorced from Colin — was pleased and proud of both her firm's performance over the frequently demanding years of the project and of Ross's diligent performance.

As for me: by carefully investing the profits from the subdivision of all my land holdings in a mixture of downtown commercial properties in Auckland and Wellington, and shares in New Zealand, Australia and Britain, Edward Maxwell Purvis, aged seventy-five, was without doubt one of the richest men in New Zealand.

Lisa and Ross's announcement.

I had liked and trusted Ross from the beginning, and the six-year project of land subdivisions and sales had justified my confidence. And while I was aware of his romantic relationship with Lisa I was surprised when she announced — at the Purvis Developments' winding up celebratory dinner — that they were getting married.

We're doing a big trip for our honeymoon, said Lisa. And *you*, daddy, she added, are going to give Ross six weeks paid leave. It was a confident daughter demand, not a request. I smiled, agreed, and stood up to shake Ross's hand and give Lisa a kiss on the cheek while

Margaret — obviously happy with the announcement — said: Oh, children, that's wonderful.

Lisa went on to say they were getting married in June and then going to Fife, in Scotland, where Ross had relatives on his mother's side. It'll be summer there, she said. Then they planned to go to Germany to see mother's family. At least the ones I've been able to contact so far, she said. First, though, she added, we're stopping over for a few days in Savannah to visit John and meet dear Minta at last. They'll be on vacation then, she said, and we're staying with them in their holiday condo in Savannah. Can't wait really.

Finally, turning to me she asked: Don't you have *any* interest in Germany and meeting Oma's family? Not really, I said, by which I meant No.

Introducing young James.

Without my noticing it, Lisa and Ross had bought one of Purvis Developments' best Brown's Bay sections, with panoramic gulf views, where they built a fine three-bedroom house. They were living there when they got married, together with Ross's fifteen-year-old son James. Margaret and I had met the lad — only in passing — but I'd never bothered to enquire about his welfare or his mother. It never occurred to me to ask although Margaret seemed to know the details. Why didn't you tell me? I asked. You didn't ask, she replied, so I thought you knew.

I learned about it only when Lisa told me she was going to be a step-mother to a teenaged boy. She told me the sad details: that Ross's first wife, whose name I forget, had died in a car crash in nineteen ninety-four. She was thirty-six years old; her little boy James, at home with his father, was eight. Ross left his job then and took a year off. To sort things out with James and everything, said Lisa.

Then he started working for you, she said.

Jesus, love, I said, I had no idea. And that's when it started? You and him? Well not straight away, said Lisa. It was slow thing. But it's good, daddy, it really is.

I knew Lisa would easily manage step-motherhood but wondered whether she was planning to have children with Ross. I wanted to ask but didn't. Lisa read my mind and told me not to worry; that she was almost too old to have children. Could be risky at my age, she said. And mummy's 'thing', you know. I grimaced at the thought. And, anyway, Lisa continued, I love my job with Wolfendale Mills, and me and Rosco are very happy the way things are.

Lisa and Ross get married.

Unlike Lisa's first wedding, her wedding to Ross was a small affair. They were married one cold Saturday afternoon in June, in the warmth of my spacious living room, by a licensed friend of Margaret, with Ross's friend Michael Something and Tui Parāone (again) as witnesses. Margaret and I were there of course together with a few of the couple's married friends; young James was both pleased and embarrassed to be there, his new haircut and new suit getting a lot of attention.

The next evening, without delay — James being looked after by his maternal grandmother in Saint Heliers — the newlyweds flew off to America for the start of six weeks of honeymooning and family reunioning.

Lisa's German family news.

They returned at last. Margaret and I visited them in Brown's Bay where we saw how happy young James was in his new home with his new stepmother.

There were sharp and bright colour photos of course, viewed on a laptop. I was especially interested in the pictures of John and Minta, sometimes with Lisa, or the four of them together, at home, in restaurants or in the streets of Savannah. Oh, daddy, said a bubbling and still-excited Lisa, it's such a *beautiful* place. I could see that for myself.

I could also see, but couldn't believe what Lisa and Ross were reporting: that John was consistently cheerful, outgoing and full of fun, and that he and Minta were devoted to each other. I wished, briefly then, that Lily could have seen the photos of her son with his lovely American wife, and her daughter with her new husband, all looking so happy.

But I was puzzled: John looked and sounded, by Lisa's report, nothing like the man I had visited in Atlanta more than ten years before. I wondered what had changed; if I had then offended John in some way I didn't know or remember. I asked Lisa: Do you think I'm in John's bad books? No, of course not, daddy, she said. Not that I know of anyway, she added quickly although I sensed something odd, evasive, about her reply.

Lisa skipped through the photos of Ross's relations in Fife; they were of no interest to me. Then she tried to engage me with the photos of mother's family in Bavaria. She pointed out and named members of a generation younger than that visited and photographed by Doris (and Ngaire) in nineteen eighty-nine although there were a few elders who remembered Doris's visit.

I still had no interest in mother's home country and family, an attitude that Lisa, Ross and Margaret couldn't understand. Lisa never again mentioned her German relatives but I assumed that she kept in contact with them.

Idle and bored, and too old for a sports car.

I was finding it difficult — even a little painful — to get in and out of my low little Mazda so I traded it in for a bright yellow Mazda 6 sedan. That's a very conservative choice, said Margaret. Except for the colour. I'm getting a bit old for a sports car, Maggie, I said. This thing'll do me just fine.

Margaret said it was the first time she'd heard me refer to my old age. I just renewed my licence, I said. Next time I'll be eighty and then I'll have to renew it every two years. This nice little job will do me just fine until then.

After years in the agency, and then working with Ross on the land subdivision projects — which included countless long meetings with council officials, town planners, contractors, bankers and, eventually, real-estate companies and their agents — I suddenly found myself idle again; and bored.

I still had my commercial properties but they demanded little attention and, anyway, Ross was exceptionally good at managing tenants; better than me by miles. Meanwhile Lisa oversaw my share portfolio and foreign cash and investments. I met with Ross (officially, that is) only once a month at the Wolfendale Mills office in Parnell where Lisa or one of her colleagues sat in to review the company's accounts and provide financial advice.

At one such meeting I learned that the rump of Ayer New Zealand — which had long ago been my own little Purvis Commercial Art — had succumbed to the failure in New York. Apparently there were only three people left in Auckland. Just an art studio really, said Lisa. I found that painfully ironic. And so, once a month, I had to sit in the Wolfendale Mills boardroom in the building

Tom Wolfendale and I had bought in nineteen sixty-one and see that my agency's part of the building — the two upper floors — was shared by three tenants. My only satisfaction came from knowing that Ayer had sold its share of the building to Wolfendale Mills which meant that Lisa — as a Wolfendale Mills partner — was now a part owner of the whole valuable building.

Anyway, by two thousand and two I was definitely bored. You need a hobby, was Margaret's suggestion. Something to keep you busy. Mind and body. New people and new ideas. I hated the idea of a hobby. Never had a hobby in my life, I said. Work's always been my hobby. I know, agreed Margaret. It's always been money, money, money hasn't it. But, Eddie, she added with a smile, believe it or not there's more to life than money.

Like what? I asked. I was only half joking.

Art as a hobby.

Reluctantly, but under pressure from Margaret, I enrolled in a daytime art class for 'seniors' which was advertised at the library and conducted in the adjacent community hall. In fact, though, I found my fellow classmates to be old and slow, unbearably dull, and utterly without talent.

I was still pretty well known then and took the attention of the tutor, a certain Matthew Fazerkerley, the owner of the somewhat controversial but successful Fazerkerley Art Academy in Grafton; he taught at the Takapuna day-class as a 'community service' he said. Something for the oldies, he said.

At the end of the first day, by which time I had already decided a suburban amateur daytime art class for 'seniors' was not for me, Fazerkerley took me aside and said: But Mr Purvis, you're not old. Actually I am, I said.

Just turned seventy-six. Well, by golly, you don't look it and you don't act it, he said. And, anyway, *this* — he waved his arm around the now messy (easels-askew, water jars, painty rags) community hall — isn't for you, and nor — as he pointed to the elderly, stooped and white-haired 'seniors' shuffling out of the room in a slow line — are they.

I nodded in silent agreement, anxious only to get out of the place.

They're just filling in time, continued Fazerkerley. Bored, nothing to do. With nil, zero, zilch artistic ability. Couldn't draw the curtains most of them. But they enjoy it and I don't mind. But *you*, Mr Purvis. You have *it*. I have no doubt. *It*. No doubt at all.

Art for money.

By the end of the following year I had been rapidly promoted through the Fazerkerley Art Academy's usual three-year course and was not only the academy's 'senior boy' —Fazerkerley's joke — but had also won the senior prize for my examination quartet — drawing with pencil, charcoal and wash, large oils on canvas, an acrylic copy of an 'old master', and a water-colour — which was the centre of the academy's end-of-year exhibition. My exhibited water-colour from that quartet — a Tybee Island scene taken from one of Lisa's American holiday photographs — was sold for a sum that was *double* anything ever achieved at a Fazerkerley graduation exhibition.

The money was no better than small change to me. What was important was the rediscovery — thanks to the eccentric but insightful Matthew Fazerkerley — of my native artistic talent which I had never developed past the easy realistic monochrome drawing for advertising. Now I discovered not only the pure pleasure of painting in colour — especially from water-colours which I decided to concentrate on — but also to discover, to my own surprise, that I could sell my paintings for money.

I've never enjoyed anything so much, I said to Margaret at the wine-and-cheese opening of the Academy's two thousand and three graduation exhibition.

More deaths.

It was while driving home from the exhibition that November night — we were in Margaret's car, she was driving — that I took a call from a weeping, sniffing Lisa which immediately dampened my cheerful mood. Sensing the importance of the call, Margaret pulled off the motorway at Onewa Road and parked as I listened and learned that Tom Wolfendale, my old friend and accountant, for so long the chief partner of Wolfendale Mills, Lisa's firm, had died suddenly at a National Party fundraising dinner.

Fifty years, I said to Margaret when the call was over. We've known each other fifty years exactly. And he was my age, exactly. Margaret resumed the drive home. We went though so much together, I continued. I couldn't have done anything without him. New York. Pan Am. He was on the board. Selling out. He got me a good price. Jesus, Maggie, I can't believe it.

I hated funerals but went to Tom Wolfendale's at Purewa where I learned that Tom's wife Dilys, who had once despised me but was permanently afflicted by Alzheimer's disease, was still alive. How bloody ironic, I said to Margaret.

It was during those happy 'art' years I learned that Bill Brown — Wiremu Parāone, Willy — had died after a minor stroke, while out fishing, followed by a major and fatal stroke in hospital. That was in the middle of two thousand and four when Willy, like me, was seventy-eight years old.

There'll be a big tangi on the Dargaville marae, said Lisa. I'm going, for Tui's sake, she said. But I didn't go. Not really up to that drive, love, I said. And all that Māori stuff. Gives me the heebie-jeebies.

It was then, too, that Lisa told me her ex-husband Colin had died in Tauranga hospital from something or other. She didn't seem too upset although it occurred to me that the poor man must have been only forty or so, Lisa's age.

What was it? I asked. Lung cancer at forty-one? said Lisa. Always a heavy smoker. Jesus Christ, I said. What next?

Painting pride comes before an exhibition fall.

Are you going to keep painting? asked Margaret. Art for art's sake and all that? Yes, I said. Absolutely. Art for art's sake. And I did. Water colours in a traditional representational style which were considered old-fashioned by many but 'exquisite' by others. I did them purely for pleasure at first although they sold regularly, through Zelnick's big Parnell Road gallery, with no effort on my part. After a year or so I decided to work towards a proper exhibition. A theme, I said to Margaret. Auckland's volcanic cones. I'm getting on for eighty, I said, so time for some proper recognition.

Again, Lisa and Margaret wanted to do something — they said 'something' without being specific — for my eightieth birthday but I wasn't interested. I had that seventieth birthday dinner thing, I said, and that was all right. I didn't mind that. Bit of fun actually. But look what's happened since, I said. Willy's dead. Tom's dead. So I don't want a dinner or a party or anything this time.

But there have been *some* good times, Eddie, said Margaret. And now, you've got your painting, and a new exhibition to look forward to. That'll do for my eightieth, I said. A successful exhibition.

But the exhibition — at a new back-street gallery in Parnell — was a failure.

It started well. The young gallery owner said such kind things about me — 'the master of the small water colour' he called me — and the hand-picked attendees seemed receptive and willing to buy. I must say I spoke well in reply. But depression set in quickly when the guests left early, leaving a gallery of unsold paintings and unconsumed food and wine. The young gallery owner — whose name and gallery I now can't and never could remember — was as depressed as I was. I knew I should have been on Parnell Road, he admitted. I agreed that Parnell Road would have been better.

Together we talked too much, drank too much and ate too little. In the end Margaret took me home, drunk, leaving the despondent gallery owner to consider his lack of experience and judgement, and his abundance of debt.

12

The collywobbles.

I recovered from my exhibition failure and eightieth birthday hangover but, for some reason, not completely. I don't know what happened that night, I said to Margaret, but I've never felt quite right since then.

I went to the doctor, a young woman Margaret recommended. They know so much when they're fresh out of medical school, she said. But she's Indian, I protested. So? asked Margaret challengingly. So nothing I suppose, I said meekly.

She was good, my new doctor, thorough and professional. She checked everything — more like a bloody vet than a doctor, I said to Margaret — and announced, at last, that I was in remarkably good health for a man of eighty. Well, I don't feel it, I said to Margaret, although I've never been eighty before. What did you tell her? she asked. I told her I couldn't explain it exactly but I've really got the collywobbles. She didn't know what I meant. Of course she didn't, said Margaret with a laugh. Collywobbles indeed.

Margaret said I was probably depressed but I angrily denied even the possibility. But the exhibition, she said. I'm not depressed about that or anything, I insisted.

Face it, Eddie, she said, the exhibition was not a complete success. That's an understatement, I said. So, a bit embarrassing? she asked. You *could* be depressed about that. But I'm not, I insisted again.

The end of art.

I'd gone to the back-street Parnell gallery to retrieve my paintings but it was closed, with no notice of explanation. I could see my paintings locked inside, still hanging in the dark. Ross tracked down the young gallery owner and reported that according to his worried partner, he — the young gallery owner — had been locked in his bedroom for days, with nothing to eat or drink, refusing to come out or talk to anyone.

Now *that's* depression, I said to Margaret.

He *did* come out, though, when Ross promised I would pay the gallery's debts if he would only let him in to retrieve my paintings. Ross then took the paintings, together with all the other paintings from my studio, finished and in-progress, and all the art paraphernalia, to a waste destruction company in one of my buildings in Papatoetoe. I then paid all the gallery's creditors, returned my north-facing studio to a guest bedroom, and never again thought of my days at Fazerkerley's and my subsequent, vain and over-confident foray into the world of professional art.

I felt better then; relieved to be rid of my painting obsession.

What a pity you couldn't have treated painting as a relaxing hobby, said Margaret. You needed a hobby then and you still do. I accepted that as probably true. My business affairs were thriving; I easily managed my financials from home — having mastered the internet — while Ross efficiently dealt with the physical properties and tenant relationships with increasing professional input from Lisa in her role at Wolfendale Mills. I was once again a fit and healthy old man with too much time on his hands.

Looking for a hobby. And the last car.

I tried bowls once. The Milford Bowling Club had an open day one fine summer Saturday and, again urged by Margaret, I went along only to learn it was a game — a skill, a talent — for which I had no aptitude. Nor did I care for the men — mostly younger than I, over-friendly and patronizing — who tried to coach me in the game. I left early and never returned.

You could have given it a bit more time, said an irritated Margaret. I should have known, I said. Balls and me don't get along. But you need to keep busy, she insisted. It's not good to have nothing to do. To be bored. And, remember, bored people become boring people.

In which connexion — seeking to avoid being both bored and boring — I began poring over Lily's extensive library which I had kept. But despite it containing the classics, old and new, of the English language, I could find nothing of interest. I couldn't help wondering how and when Lily managed to read, understand and appreciate so much writing which I found so dense.

For the same reason — to find something interesting to do connected to Lily — I dipped into her record collection of vinyl LPs which included all the great composers as well as rock classics from our generation. I still had an old-fashioned stereo but I didn't know what of Lily's classical music to play nor, when I played it, what I should be listening for. I did play some of her old rock albums but thought they sounded dated; and, anyway, they reminded me too much of her.

But, daddy, said Lisa when she realized I had kept

Lily's record collection. Those old vinyls would be worth a fortune now. And that stereo. But I wasn't interested. They can all stay there, I said. When I'm gone you can do what you like with them.

In two thousand and ten, just before my eighty-fourth birthday, I failed to pass my driving test. My clever Indian lady doctor said my eyesight just wasn't good enough. Annoyed, and now conveniently doubting her ability, I got a second opinion from an expensive young optometrist who only confirmed my doctor's opinion. Resigned, then, to giving up driving, I sold my car; my bright yellow Mazda-6 which still looked good and was running perfectly despite being more than eight years old.

The North Shore Residents' Club.

I joined the North Shore Residents' Club. It wasn't an especially 'good' club but it was close to my apartment, overlooking the beach, which meant I could easily walk to and from there, even at night, which was important without a car.

I had hoped to meet interesting local people there but it was a vain hope. I was disappointed to learn — again — that my world was now full of boring, old, mostly white people, more women than men, who for unknown reasons were full of resentment and indignation, with strange and reactionary attitudes towards young people, climate change, crime, the Labour party, Chinese immigrants, Māoris and more; attitudes I had rarely encountered in business where people were too busy to be prejudiced, judgemental or worried about things they couldn't change.

Margaret, too, joined the club which was just as well; she was more tolerant. She said she could see all sorts of fear behind people's front; she managed to find goodness and kindness where I had seen stupidity and simmering resentment. You have to understand, she said, that a lot of old people who live alone get plain *lonely*. They have no one to talk to all day, and nothing to talk about. They listen to all the cranks on talk-back radio and think those opinions are normal. So when they're in company they talk incessantly, from an empty head, about nothing.

Eddie Purvis, the old bore.

Despite Margaret's generous attitude I still found most of the club's members boring so I was shocked when she told me, bluntly, that *I* was becoming an old bore — just like them — especially when I regaled others with my financial affairs, business experience and international travels with Pan Am.

If you're not careful people will start avoiding *us* soon, she said. It was a lesson I needed to learn. As a result I became more tolerant, treating the club as the focus of my social life.

For the next few years I again settled into a routine I once would have considered slow, dull and repetitive but, as I approached ninety, found reassuringly predictable. I still dressed well and looked after my appearance although towards the end of that decade I became a little stooped. My spectacles were a bit thicker but my hearing, assisted by my minute and almost invisible aids, had not deteriorated further. And I still had my own teeth.

I shopped for myself, Margaret driving her car and doing her own shopping as she helped me. I still prepared and ate a good breakfast and, except for the two or three nights a week at the club, prepared my own dinner. Lunch was usually a simple snack either at the club or in a local cafe while out with Margaret.

Nothing — and no one — lasts forever.

Altogether then, at that time, for those few years, I was truly and consciously content. But such easy contentment couldn't and didn't last although I was shocked when it came to a jarring, shuddering stop.

You shouldn't be surprised, Eddie, said Margaret weakly with an equally weak pretend smile. Nothing lasts forever. You should know that by now. So you take care of yourself. Promise?

Those were the last words I heard from my dear old friend who died from complications arising from a mysterious cancer which seemed to have come on suddenly.

Don't be silly, she said when she told me about it. It's not a sudden thing. Cancers don't just happen. It must have been there all the time only I didn't know. But what is it? I asked; I was puzzled and frightened to see her looking so thin and wan and weak so quickly after her diagnosis. It's a woman's thing, Eddie she said, turning her head on the pillow and smiling grimly. Don't worry. It's not contagious.

Margaret Mary Carrucan died nine weeks later in the Takapuna hospice to which she had given so much of her own time and money for so many years. It was peaceful and painless passing, thanks to modern pain relief, in the early hours of Sunday the sixteenth of August, twenty fifteen. She was eighty-two years old.

Lisa was distraught. She had visited Margaret in the hospital and then the hospice — where it was assumed she was the patient's daughter — every day during the weeks of her confinement and had cried after every visit. But we were both excluded from any mourning or funeral arrangements by Margaret's remaining siblings who apparently had disapproved of her friendship with the rich, greedy and non-Catholic Eddie Purvis and his family. Margaret had warned me of that. Nevertheless, Lisa and I attended the requiem mass — which we found long, impersonal and ridiculous — despite being snubbed by every one of Margaret's extended family. We didn't go to the cemetery.

Actually I'm sure Margaret wanted to be cremated, I said.

Painful forgotten memories.

It took a lot of sleuthing by Lisa, later, to learn exactly where Margaret was buried in the sprawling Schnapper Rock cemetery. She took me there one Saturday afternoon a few weeks later; we laid flowers on the grave. You know, I said as we walked away, I think your mother's buried here somewhere.

Lisa was shocked. Mummy was cremated, daddy. Don't you remember? We stopped and sat on a bench with views of the upper harbour. I turned to Lisa feeling a bit bewildered; confused. Who arranged it all, your mother's funeral? I asked. I don't remember anything about it. You were in no state, daddy, said Lisa. Me and Aunt Dossy and Ngaire did everything. Ngaire was good. She knew what to do. I don't remember, I said again. We told you *everything*, daddy, said Lisa. We really did. And you agreed.

I looked out across the sloping expanse of the vast cemetery. So where's her grave? I asked. There's no grave, daddy. Remember? She was *cremated*. There's a wee place for her ashes in the memorial wall. Room for you too if you like. Ngaire arranged that. Where is it, this wall? I asked. Come on, said Lisa as she stood up. I looked up at her. Suddenly I felt especially old. I must have looked it too as Lisa put out her hand to steady me. I took her arm then and we set off up the sealed path.

Isn't it awful, I said. It's all new to me. I don't remember anything. I'm only here because of Margaret.

Lisa led me to that section of wall where Lily's gritty remains lay in a slate box behind a brass plaque. Lilian Dawn Purvis (Braithwaite). Dearly beloved... I could hardly bear to read the plaque. But I did. Silently. We walked slowly back to Lisa's car. Again I depended on Lisa's arm.

Suddenly I stopped and asked: But where's your grandmother? Lisa smiled sadly. Daddy, she said patiently, don't you remember? Aunt Ngaire arranged to have her and Grandfather Quentin and little Catherine-Anne put together in a special place at Waikumete. So much death I thought, not for the first time. Grace is there too, said Lisa. At Waikumete. And Aunt Dossy and Ngaire.

I remember now, I said. But I didn't. I blew a long breath through pursed lips before adding: Anyway, we better go.

Margaret was good friend, you know, love, I said. But I really *loved* your mother. Really. With all my heart. And now, after all these years — I stopped and waved back vaguely in the direction of Lily's wall — I feel so ashamed. Don't worry, daddy, said Lisa kindly. I come here often for us.

But what about your grandmother and the rest of them? I go to Waikumete too, said Lisa. I always take flowers. For them all. From us. Me and you and John. They'd understand you know. They really would. I shook my head slowly. Thank you, love, I said.

And then, suddenly, I felt broken, emotionally and physically.

Introducing Sylvan Park.

Lisa must have noticed my sudden brokenness because

she didn't seem surprised when, a couple of weeks later, during a Sunday visit, I told her I was selling the apartment and moving to Sylvan Park. It was a cold October afternoon and we — Ross was there too — were sitting inside. It's all arranged, I said. The agent said she'll have no trouble selling the apartment and I've signed up for a nice place at Sylvan Park. Just one bedroom. That's all I need now. There's care there too if I need it.

I wasn't entirely happy with my decision but I had no choice: Margaret was gone and, to be honest, I wasn't really coping on my own. Lisa *appeared* to approve — surely she would — but I wasn't sure she was being sincere. You'll have lots of company there, daddy, she said a little too brightly. And they'll take care of you. I guessed she was a little hurt that I'd made my decision without confiding in her. I wished then that I had because she was the only person in the world who cared for me. *The only one.* There was Ross and young James, of course, but they were different. And I never heard from John. In fact I'd given up emailing him; I got whatever news there was, of John and Minta, from Lisa.

Anyway, I should be there by Christmas, I said, trying to sound enthusiastic. Perhaps we'll have Christmas dinner there. Together. In my new place.

Awful news from Atlanta.
We didn't have Christmas dinner at Sylvan Park. I cancelled everything: the Takapuna apartment was taken off the market; and, while the Sylvan Park purchase was completed, I wasn't up to the stress of the move.

Because only a week after telling Lisa and Ross of my decision to move, Lisa phoned me — it was the next Sunday, Labour weekend — and said she had to see me at once. She sounded upset. I waited anxiously. She arrived at last. We sat outside on the terrace while a pale and shocked-looking Lisa — with Ross at her side on the two-seater — told me that my son, her brother, John Purvis, who lived in far-away Atlanta — had died suddenly the day before, Friday in America.

Lisa burst into tears then, and seemed oblivious to Ross's comforting arm, while I merely stared at my daughter in shocked disbelief. After many silent minutes I managed to ask feebly: It wasn't the *myotonic dystrophy* thing was it? Lisa shook her head vigorously, flicking tears off her cheeks in the process. Heart, she said. His bloody heart.

Later, when Lisa and Ross had gone, I was able to calmly step through the sequence of events which Lisa had, through tears and sniffs, laid out for me. Evidently Minta had phoned her with the news early that morning. Minta said he was with the college track team the day before, at a Friday afternoon track meet somewhere, when he had simply collapsed while jogging alongside and coaching the warming-up relay team. He was rushed to the hospital but died in the ambulance from a massive heart attack.

But he was so fit and healthy, I said. An athlete for God's sake. I don't know, daddy, Lisa said, sniffingly. These things happen don't they. Even the fittest people. But you'd think they would have known, I said angrily. Don't they do medicals and things in America? A big university. Health insurance and all that American bullshit. I was angry then.

Lisa could only shake her head grimly before wiping her eyes and blowing her nose. Who can explain it, daddy? It's so sad. It's bloody awful, I said. Poor Minta, said Lisa.

John Maxwell Purvis was fifty-five years old.

Many moving tributes.

Minta sent Lisa a video file of John's funeral but I was reluctant to see it. But you *should*, daddy, she said. All the tributes from his friends and colleagues and students. It's so lovely. Really. You'd be so moved. And proud.

I watched on Lisa's laptop. And, yes, I was moved. And proud. But I still couldn't reconcile the John *I* knew with the John Purvis, Athletics Director, who was evidently, very obviously, loved, admired, respected, by everyone who spoke to the large congregation — many were weeping — in the big church.

He went to church? I was astonished to learn that John was a 'dearly beloved' member of the Something Baptist Church of Something who would be 'sadly missed' by everyone there. He was never religious, I said. Never *ever*. That's when Ross said: You *have* to belong to a church if you work in a school or university in the Southern states. Otherwise you wouldn't get a job. Wouldn't even get an interview. But look, I said then. They're all black people. It's Minta's church, said Lisa. John joined her church.

I shook my head slowly. My son was a complete mystery. Evidently everyone loved him (except me, I thought) and he loved everyone (except me, I thought again).

Good tidings at Christmas.

By Christmas, by which time I thought I'd be entertaining Lisa, Ross and James for Christmas dinner at Sylvan Park, I was still in Takapuna. Lisa picked me up and took me back to Brown's Bay.

Where's young James? I asked. He's not 'young James' anymore, daddy, said Lisa. He's twenty-nine. Really? I was astonished. Not only that, continued Lisa, but he's got a partner. Lucie. They even have a wee kiddie, a boy. Called Ross. Isn't that nice. They live in Wellington now.

How come I didn't know all that? I asked. We did tell you, daddy, said Lisa gently. You must have forgotten. So you're a grandmother, I said. I like to think so, said Lisa glancing at Ross who smiled and nodded. So what does he do in Wellington? I asked. Well, said Ross, he's an accountant. A very successful accountant, added Lisa, if I may say so. I liked that.

Much more was discussed at that very pleasant Christmas dinner: family; my childhood; my parents; my Uncle Toby; Doris (and Ngaire) and little Catherine-Ann; the many German relations that Lisa knew but I didn't; dear Lily; Margaret; even Lisa's partnership at Wolfendale Mills, and the new Purvis Holdings and Developments over which Ross and Lisa now had complete control. John was mentioned only in passing; Lisa referred more often to 'poor Minta' and told me they kept in touch. I think she might retire soon, she said.

The old man in the mirror.

One Saturday in April — the day after my ninetieth (uncelebrated) birthday, a long weekend for ANZAC day — I was again ready to move to Sylvan Park; I was waiting, impatiently I must admit, for Lisa and Ross to pick me up.

Unfortunately, in the six months since John's death my health had deteriorated. It wasn't a stroke or a heart attack or anything catastrophic but it was enough to slow me down and cause me (and Lisa too) more anxiety about my health than I (or she) had ever had. I kept getting dizzy. Felt like I was going to fall over. Vertigo, said the doctor. Buy a walking stick, she said. It'll give you a bit more confidence. I came to use my stick, came to rely on it for 'confidence', just as the doctor had said.

I noticed then, when I saw myself in the full length mirrored-glass doors of the terrace, as I went out there to wait for Lisa, that I was walking with a more-than-slight stoop, even when using my stick. I paused and properly studied my bent self. Look at me, I thought. A bent over old man, in a thick overcoat that's too big but still feeling the cold, leaning forward on my walking stick. My white hair's all thin and wispy now, and blowing all over the place in the light breeze. A wrinkled brow, bushy eyebrows over thick glasses, a permanent frown, looking a bit angry around the moist mouth. An old, old man. Can't deny it.

But, bugger it, in my head I still felt — still feel, now — like the young, tall, fashionable, clever, quick-witted, rich and successful, well-dressed and well-groomed advertising man-of-the-world I once was. So long ago. If only they'd known me then. If only they knew where I've been, what I've seen, who I've met, what I've done. If only.

By 'they' I meant everyone. But no one cares and that's a fact.

And then, as I was about to sit down to wait for Lisa, the doorbell rang. It seemed to echo harshly, impatiently, in the empty apartment.

13

Lisa, Ross and...

At last: Lisa and Ross had arrived. I stepped inside, closed the terrace door awkwardly, crossed the empty living room slowly, using my stick, and opened the door, ready to leave, only to be suddenly pounced upon. In my fright, as I dropped my stick, I saw Lisa and Ross standing behind the pouncer, in the hall, smiling. Why were they smiling?

Father-in-law, said Minta Purvis loudly as she released me from her arms and stood back. Oh, my God, I said, struggling for a moment to even remember my daughter-in-law's name. What the hell?

Just as Minta looked at me, I looked at her, trying to take it all in; her surprising presence. I saw she was crying. Not howling or sobbing; just weeping. Weeping and *smiling* at the same time. Why? I wondered.

In her arms, and then standing apart, I felt small and thin and frail. She looked taller than I recalled but I quickly, ruefully, remembered my stooped and shrunken reflection in the mirrored terrace door. And as she wiped her cheeks with the back of her hands, sniffing and half-laughing and sort-of jumping up and down with joy — *really* — before reaching to the floor to retrieve my stick, I thought consciously that she looked absolutely — the most apt word I could think of — BEAUTIFUL.

She was tall, elegant and, yes, beautiful. She was dressed in bright yellow and red outfit which I can't really describe. A pant suit perhaps. Is that still a 'thing' women wear? Anyway, her skin was brown and smooth, her lips were red, her teeth (she was still smiling) were bright white, her moist eyes were black, her hair was thick and curly and shiny but no longer entirely black, and she was obviously — to my surprise — really glad to see me.

She was glad to see *me*. I couldn't believe it. She stood back then, spread her arms, her palms up, and said, in her soft and distinctive Southern accent: I come all the way to see you, father-in-law. Here I am. Aint you glad to see the girl?

I thought then how lucky John had been to meet and marry such a person. Daddy, called Lisa over Minta's shoulder. Say something. Aren't you glad to see Minta? Oh, I am, I said. I *really* am.

And then, suddenly, I felt dizzy. I have to sit down, I said. There was no furniture in the room, nothing to sit on but the floor. Ross stepped forward, between Lisa and Minta, who both looked worried but helpless, to steady me until the blackness and vertigo went away.

Minta in New Zealand.

Minta stayed with Lisa and Ross in Brown's Bay for three weeks and so shared the low-key and belated celebration of my ninetieth birthday. She also made a two-day trip to Dunedin to not only see John's university — although that seemed important — but also to catch up with some scientist at Otago she knew through her past collaboration with Stephen Hawking.

Before she left New Zealand, though, she spent a lot of time talking with me and Lisa. She wanted to know *everything* about John and his family. Lisa took her to the cemeteries — Schnapper Rock and Waikumete — to see the family graves and plots; Lisa told me she photographed all the plaques and headstones.

She spent a lot of time with me at Sylvan Park but also in some local cafes and coffee shops. It's nice to get out, father-in-law, she said. She had Lisa's car and had discovered Devonport. She took me there often where, if it was fine, we'd get out and sit on a bench to look across to the city, watch the ferries, big container ships and cruise liners, coming and going, and talk. I tried to explain what it was like for me there, in Devonport, as a poor bare-footed boy, hitching a ride from town on the slow old steam ferries. But Minta was more interested in John's growing up in Minehaha — wealthy and spoiled according to what he had told her — information she added to that provided by Lisa.

Only then did she ask about my wider family, my Kiwi father and German mother, about Doris (and Ngaire) and Catherine-Ann, which seemed to make sense to her having visited the two cemeteries. There was so much to tell; stuff I hadn't thought about for years.

The unsolved mystery of John Maxwell Purvis.
But I had my own questions of Minta. I discovered, in her answers, that John's attitude — concerning family matters — was as much a mystery to her as it was to me.

I tell y'all the truth, she said to me one breezy day, as we sat together on the Devonport sea wall, and I said the same to Lisa. I never heard John say a bad word about y'all, specially you, father-in-law. But, she added, I never heard him say a good word either, and that's a goddam fact. What about his mother? I asked hopefully, but Minta merely shook her head slowly. Strange, aint it, she said. It's not natural, for a boy or a man, but he never said nothing about her either. Not ever.

John's strange attitude to his family, to his past in New Zealand, remains a mystery I've never solved.

The constant churn of the old.

The next few years passed peacefully for me if not for the world. I settled comfortably into an institutional-style life here at Sylvan Park and even made a couple of friends amongst the residents I once scorned. They're all so bloody old, I said to Lisa, adding that they were mostly women and mostly miserable.

But even my friendships — including, in the beginning, a lawyer and an accountant who reminded me of my old friends Reece Williams and Tom Wolfendale, both younger than me — were short-lived. But, anyway, as one old professional died he was inevitably replaced by another of the same ilk. It was a constant churn I came to accept as natural and inevitable. One day, I knew, it would be my turn to go and be replaced.

The weeks and months passed, turning into years, but I didn't really care or worry. Sometimes I wasn't even sure what day it was until I checked the *Herald*. It often puzzled me that I could remember every detail of my tenth birthday — my little *Bifora* watch — but couldn't remember what I had for breakfast. Before long I found myself spending more time in the room they moved me to.

This room. I like being here on my own.

Reliable Lisa.

Lisa continues to visit and is always willing to take me out. But while the frequency of her visits remains the same the frequency of our outings has gradually reduced. I was pretty mobile until recently but I don't go out much now; I've come to depend more and more on the frame thing they gave me.

Lisa, Ross and the staff are impressed that I haven't become rude or impatient. In fact I try hard to project a calm resignation, being always kind and polite. Actually I rarely feel calm or resigned, kind or polite, but I know how people dislike impatient, ill-tempered and ungrateful old men. I'm determined not to be branded one of them but it isn't easy. Being a benign old gentleman is plain hard work.

It's turned out to be pretty good here really, I said to Lisa one day after Minta had left. That's when they moved me into this new room. I told her: I don't have to do anything. Someone comes in and makes the bed every day, I said. Helps me shower sometimes, cleans the place every Friday before the weekend. And my dinner gets delivered every night. It's really good.

I don't know who arranged it all but it suits me fine. I don't have to do a thing.

Lisa tried to explain something then but I wasn't really interested. A bit tired I suppose. I am these days. Sometimes Ross comes with Lisa and talks business. He thinks he should keep me up to date with the company's affairs but I have to pretend to be interested.

Introducing Allison.

One day, more than a year ago now, out of the blue, there was a nice young lady about Lisa's age in my room telling me how famous and important I was and that she'd be ever so grateful — and so would the university and the library and the people of New Zealand, and apparently the whole bloody world if I believed her — if I would learn to work the little black plastic thing she had brought with her. This thing here, she said. Turn it on and off with this, and speak into it here, and just ramble on, in your own time, your own words, about your memories of Auckland, what New Zealand was like, growing up and being in business, having a family, when you retired, all that sort of thing. No one will care about all that, I said to Allison. That was her name. Actually I was flattered but was hoping to sound modest.

Something strange was going on but I didn't know what.
And so it began and continued, on and off, for a year or more — can't remember exactly — until my contentment, born of a safe and predictable routine, was rudely disturbed by what I saw and heard on the news supported by chatter from the staff and other residents. It didn't make any sense and I became annoyed.

What the bloody hell are they talking about? I asked Lisa angrily one evening. What the hell's going on? Don't worry about it, daddy, she said, trying to calm me down. It's not important. It won't affect you. I *do* worry about it, I insisted. The talk is everywhere but I don't know what the hell it's all about.

What they were talking about — what the whole country was talking about — was an apparently deadly pandemic. What a bloody palaver. Next thing all the staff were wearing full length gowns and clear plastic masks that made them look like astronauts. And when they weren't wearing all that paraphernalia they wore blue papery masks over their mouth and nose so that I couldn't even recognize them or understand what the hell they were saying. Especially the Asian ones. Hard enough to understand *them* anyway.

Lisa phoned that first day and told me she wouldn't be able to visit for a while. Not allowed. For how long?

I asked. I don't know, daddy. I really don't. But I need my lollies and Mallow Puffs and TV Guide and a new puzzle book, I said. And I never get the paper anymore. And all Lisa could say was: Daddy, I'm *so* sorry but it's just not allowed. Even me and Ross. We have to stay home. Can't go anywhere. Bloody hell, I said. Oh, daddy, I'm *so so* sorry, Lisa said again. I could tell she was crying. Properly crying.

That was my daughter on the phone, I said to the all-covered-up cleaning woman who was in my toilet but didn't want to talk. I tell you what, I continued anyway, she's the only person in the world — the only person in the whole bloody world — who cares anything for me. And yet that bloody prime minister bitch won't let her come and see me. Even on my birthday. I turned ninety-four just the other day. Same day as the queen. Twenty-first of April, nineteen twenty-six. Both of us ninety-four. My birthday, and my only child — my only family in the world — she couldn't come and see me. I could die and she wouldn't be allowed. Wouldn't even be allowed at my funeral. That's if I'm *allowed* to have a funeral.

I'm sorry, Mr Purvis, said the masked cleaner as she left the room pushing her trolley of cleaning equipment and chemicals out the door. She didn't even look back at me.

I was angry.

I survived that stupid covid lockdown but there were some around here who didn't. They were pretty sick old buggers anyway, I said to Lisa when she came to visit at last.

But *you're* all right, daddy, she said. That's the main thing isn't it? I suppose so, I said grudgingly. But I tell you what, love, I added, I watched that girly prime minister on television, and that skinny little lackey bureaucrat standing beside her, and she's a *fake*. A complete fake. All kind and gentle and feminine and lovey-dovey but behind that big toothy smile she's as hard as nails. Believe me. *Hard*. And heartless. Because all through this lockdown thing — I've watched it on telly — nothing but cruelty. You couldn't visit me but that was nothing compared with people — kids too — dying of cancer. Then no funerals. In here too. Real sick. But not allowed visitors. Kiwis not allowed to come home to their own country. People being forced to have injections they don't want. That sounds like a cruel, heartless dictatorship to me.

Credit to Lisa: she listened patiently to my grumpy old man opinions, without argument, saying only: She means well, daddy. She really does.

And then, suddenly, I remembered. One good thing happened though, I said. What's that? asked Lisa, probably relieved I had changed the subject. All those weeks I couldn't see you, I said. It was so quiet around here. I picked up Allison's little recording machine, which was lying beside me, on my bed, and waved it in her face. I had time to work on my story, I said.

Oh, daddy, said Lisa, that's amazing. All this time you've been doing it? Just about every day, a bit, I said. I'll properly finish it tonight. Then I need to get hold of that Allison woman. I'll do that, daddy, said Lisa. I was surprised. Do you know how to get in touch with her? Yes, daddy, she said. I know. She's a friend of mine remember. She's the one who asked me about you. Whether you'd do it for her.

Oh, that's right, I said. I remember now. But I didn't.

I told Lisa I'd finish it tonight — which I'm doing right now — so she can have it tomorrow and give it to that Allison.

She'll be so glad you managed to do it, said Lisa when she kissed me goodnight.

And that's it. The end of what I did.

Editor's note: This is a transcription of the recording made by Mr Purvis over almost two years. It has been edited lightly, where necessary, and broken down into readable sections, but is otherwise true to the original voice recording. Of course we have no way of knowing what else Mr Purvis did — what he omitted from his story — which must have helped shape his life and affected the lives of those around him, but it is nevertheless an invaluable record of Auckland's social and business history.

Mr Purvis made the recording at the behest of his daughter, the noted Auckland arts patron and philanthropist, Dame Lisa Tayloe (ONZ, DBE), to whom the university is especially grateful. The original recording is stored in the university's oral history archives and a digital copy has been lodged with the research department of the Auckland Public Library.

Mr Purvis was born on the same day as Queen Elizabeth II (26th of April, 1926). She, however, outlived him by a couple of years; he died peacefully, in his sleep, on the 5th of July, 2020, aged 94, not long after completing his spoken story and just before Auckland's second pandemic lockdown.

Allison Kirkharle (Professor)
Director of New Zealand Social History
History Department, University of Auckland
2023

THE END